Veryan, Walk 5

AROUND
MEVAGISSEY

St Ewe, Walk 10

Trenowth Mill, Walk 2

First published 1992 by
LANDFALL PUBLICATIONS
Landfall, Penpol, Devoran, Truro, Cornwall TR3 6NW
Telephone Truro (0872) 862581

Copyright © R.S.Acton, 1992

A CIP catalogue record for this book is available from the British Library.

ISBN 1 873443 04 8

All rights reserved. No part of this book may be reproduced or transmitted in any form or by any means including recording or photocopying, without prior permission in writing from the publisher.

IMPORTANT NOTE

I have done my best to ensure that all the recommended routes are on public rights of way, with a few unavoidable exceptions mentioned in the text, and that they are all unobstructed. If you come across unexpected difficulties (new fences, changed field-boundaries, rotted footbridges, waist-deep mud ....) please be patient, take the nearest practicable alternative route, and if possible let me know about the problem so that I can refer to it in any future edition of this book. Please help farmers and other landowners by leaving all gates as you found them, and by keeping dogs on a lead when there are livestock nearby.

USING THE BOOK

The boxed note at the start of each walk description is intended to be read before you set out; sometimes it would be useful to make preparations a day or two in advance in order to get the most out of the walk. A star (*) indicates that there is a boxed note on this point - usually but not always on the same page. The directions attempt to be very exact and explicit, but the maps are only rough sketches, so I'd strongly recommend taking with you the relevant Ordnance Survey maps. Landranger 204 (Truro, Falmouth & surrounding area) covers all of the routes. Best of all for walkers is the Pathfinder series; the sheets named "Mevagissey and Tregony", "Falmouth and St Mawes" and "St Austell and Fowey" are the relevant ones.

Typesetting, maps, drawings and photographs by Bob Acton

Printed by the Troutbeck Press
and bound by R. Booth Ltd., Antron Hill, Mabe, Penryn, Cornwall

INTRODUCTION

You may be wondering why this book is called *Around Mevagissey*, since the village of that name is very much on the edge of the territory concerned. The fact is that my original plan was to include the coast as far east as Par, but as the work progressed it became obvious that there were too many fine walks in the area to be contained in a book of reasonable dimensions. One sunny November day when I was exploring the delightful countryside around Tregrehan Mills I finally decided to hive off all the routes at the north-eastern corner and make another book of them, to be called *Around St Austell*. I suppose the next step ought to have been to drop my first title and call the other book *Around Portholland* or *Around Tregony*, but somehow neither seems to have the same appeal, attractive and interesting though both those places are! So ten walks were given a new home, and the ten that remain still make quite a substantial collection. One of the main reasons for that is the considerable historical interest of some of the routes, particularly those around St Stephen, Grampound and Tregony. I am very conscious of the fact that much of the coast in this area has been well described in attractive and very reasonably priced leaflets produced by the National Trust and the South Cornwall Heritage Coast. For me to attempt to compete directly with them would be foolish and futile; that is one reason why I have paid so much attention to inland Cornwall, whilst still of course including the whole of the coast path from Portscatho to Pentewan in the walks. A more important reason is the attractiveness and historical richness, not only of the three inland places I have just mentioned but also of Probus, Trewithen, Philleigh, Golden, Veryan, St Ewe ..... Follow the fledgling Fal! Discover prehistoric hill forts! Explore ten medieval churches! (Having just drawn sketches of the whole lot I can vouch for the unique design of every one.) Trace the relics of a (nearly) forgotten industry! ..... That's more than enough advertising slogans. I hope even those who know the region well will make a few discoveries with the help of this book.

ACKNOWLEDGEMENTS

Although only one of the walks features much in the way of "industrial archaeology", I again owe a debt of gratitude to Kenneth Brown and Charles Thurlow of the Trevithick Society for checking and where necessary correcting my references to mining, china clay and china stone. Several others have also given valuable help with the St Stephen walk, notably John Yeo of Terras Mill, John Hawkins of Hawkins Motors, and Courtenay Smale and Jack Goldsworthy of the Goonvean and Rostowrack China Clay Co. I also want to thank the Revs. Michael Geach and John Rham for information about Veryan and St Ewe parishes, Maisie and Ivor Herring for giving my wife and me a guided tour of Heligan house and grounds, and Joanna Mattingly of the Royal Cornwall Museum for leading me to Charles Henderson's notes and supplying several interesting "snippets" about Tregony and other places. If I seem to have forgotten the help *you* gave, please forgive me - but it may be that you are mentioned in the main text, along with the many authors whose books, leaflets, articles and unpublished writings I have drawn upon.

D. C. Acton - January 1992

WALK 1
AROUND PROBUS:
TWO SHORT WALKS
OR ONE OF MEDIUM LENGTH

South of the village: about three miles   North: under two miles
The two combined: nearly four-and-a-half miles

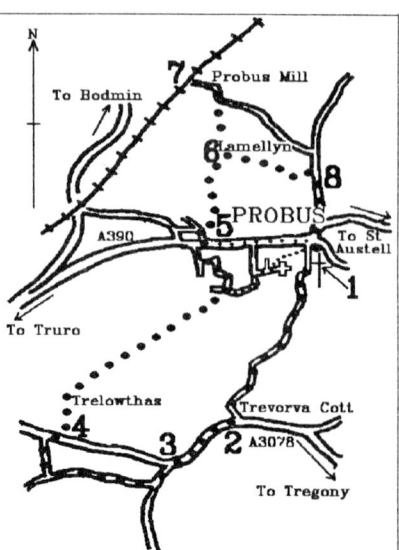

Probus is an ancient and interesting village ("almost a town", as Betjeman remarks) which is pleasant to explore, despite the ghastly through traffic (but see the first boxed note regarding the prospects for a bypass). The church is magnificent, and one of the main pleasures of walking through the undulating countryside of what was known as "the garden parish of the county" is the variety of views you get of the church. In addition to that, there are three quite large farms on the route, one of which has an ancient cross and another a very attractive farmhouse. The walk on the north side also visits the site of a watermill, but you will need a strong imagination to reconstruct the scene as it was when the mill worked. The paths around Probus are generally quite well maintained, with clear signs and good stiles and footbridges. You may need to walk through a ploughed and planted field at Trelowthas farm, and there are some spots where mud is likely. There are few steep hills to trouble you. The southern walk includes about 350 m. along the A3078 road, but I don't think you should let that put you off. Probus has a pub, the Hawkins Arms, where we found the atmosphere friendly, and the food was tasty, inexpensive and quick to appear. The garden has (or did have, in 1991) a children's play area, a splendid view of the church tower and a very elegant and well-mannered Great Dane. There are also at least two shops selling provisions, and a surprisingly large number of restaurants, tea-rooms and the like.

Probus (*) is a couple of miles west of Grampound on the main St Austell - Truro road (A390). It is often possible to park in the village square (or, to be pedantic, triangle) beside the church, but your car would be safer from bumps and less likely to impede other vehicles if you used the car park beside the village hall, which is on a small side-road to the left (driving towards Truro) a little way past the church. Probus is served by buses from St Austell and Truro (not Sundays). The walk directions begin at the churchyard's main entrance on the square. FOR THE WALK ON THE NORTH SIDE OF THE VILLAGE, start reading near the end of section 4.

PROBUS

The Demonstration Gardens and the church tower are probably nowadays the only celebrated features of Probus, but time was when it had two other claims to fame: as a centre of learning, and, by way of contrast, as the setting for fairs and "sports". Those quotation marks were prompted by an account written by a visitor to Probus in 1855, William White, who witnessed what the local "loungers" called a "wrostlin' day". "At the first note of the drum and clarinet I walked up to the field where the ring was formed on the smooth turf, and where each tavern had an improvised tap, with casks of ale, bottles of spirits, and pipes and tobacco, all in readiness. A considerable number of spectators were already seated on the forms round the ring, some of them none the better for drink, and a few lying in drunken sleep in the ring, all the worse." The Cornish "wrestlers" entered the ring and stripped almost naked. "A party of well-dressed women standing near me on the bank", notes William with surprise, "looked on with perfect composure." The wrestling did not impress him, and he comments that it "seemed to me more a speculation of the two tavern keepers than the emulous recreation of a parish." H.L.Douch, who includes White's account in *Old Cornish Inns* (1966), also mentions that an estimated 6,000 people attended the Probus Games in 1818. Hurling flourished at Probus: in 1863, for instance, *The West Briton* announced a forthcoming Hurling Match, Probus *versus* The County. According to Polsue, the author of *Lake's Parochial History* (1873), "considerable fairs" were held at Probus each year on April 5 and 23, July 5 and September 17. Such occasions are still fresh in the memory of some of the village's older inhabitants; so too is Probus School, founded in 1852 as a boys' boarding school, which is described by Polsue as "an excellent classical and mathematical school". One of its prized possessions was a letter from Captain Scott thanking the school for money it had raised in 1912: one of the sledges he used on his last expedition was named Probus. The school closed in 1960 when the headmaster, pursued by his creditors, left in too great a hurry to remember his pyjamas. By 1964 the building, which Betjeman calls "a splendid composition", was already "standing overgrown and forgotten"; a garage occupies the site now. In fact, the importance of Probus in the world of education goes back much further: the grammar school "anciently established here" had "long ceased to exist" by the time Polsue wrote. Probus produced one of the few Cornish composers to achieve fame: Giles Farnaby .... not exactly a name to conjure with, I admit, but a favourite writer and performer of madrigals and keyboard pieces at the court of Elizabeth I. The principal landed gentry of Probus parish are written about in the notes on Walk 3: the Hawkins family of Trewithen (who also played a major part in the history of Pentewan: see *Around St Austell*, Walk 6) and the Wolvedons and Tregians of Golden Manor. As for the future of Probus, the greatest and most desirable development will be the diverting of the main road that slices it in half. The promised bypass has already been postponed and rerouted more than once; the current plan is for a new road on the south side to be built in 1994-5. If and when it materialises it may well interfere with the walk route I have suggested.

WALK 1

1 FOR THE SOUTHERN WALK, go through the churchyard. If the church (*) is open, it's well worth a visit. In any case, go round to the far side of it for the walk, leaving the churchyard by the south gate. An alternative attractive route for the start of the walk is to use Wagg Lane; this runs close beside the great tower and takes you past an old pump which in the opinion of J.Meyrick marks the most likely site of the Holy Well of Saints Probus and Grace. In either case, you continue more-or-less straight ahead along a minor road. Ignore the left turning, Ridgeway. Soon the road becomes a lane, and gradually it deteriorates into a rough track, fully justifying the warning, "Unsuitable for Motor Vehicles." (The equivalent notice at the far end reads, "Unsuitable for Heavy Goods Vehicles", which seems distinctly misleading.) The hedges on both sides are high, but occasionally the wide view to the right reveals itself; and although this track links two main roads, you feel miles away from traffic for most of its length. There is one fairly stiff climb, at the top of which you are compensated by a good view back to Probus. Eventually you will come to Trevorva Cott Farm and the A3078 road to Tregony and the Roseland.

2 Turn right on the main road. For most of the approximately 350 m. of it that you have to walk you can use the verge on the right, although it is a bit rough and may be thickly vegetated. Luckily, this road is not usually very busy, but the traffic does tend to be fast. You need to cross to the left side eventually, and it is probably best to do so at or near the end of the layby, because it is much harder to see approaching traffic at the corner.

3 Take the first left turning, signposted to Tresawle, Merther and St Michael Penkivel, and then almost immediately turn right on to a quiet little road running parallel to the main one, following the sign to St Michael Penkivel. Just past West Trelowthas Bungalow, turn right, and then on returning to the A-road turn right again.

4 After a mercifully short distance, cross and turn left, following a footpath sign at the entrance to Trelowthas Manor. Notice the old cross on your right, apparently carved in slate. Trelowthas was the site of one of the eight chapels of Probus collegiate church, and there are the remains of a holy well close to the farm buildings, but not visible from the public footpaths. (See Meyrick, p.127-8.) Go straight on past the new-looking house, among the concrete buildings and tall silos (not quite what the word "manor" leads one to expect), and take the signed footpath going to the right. The path now heads more-or-less towards the church tower (just slightly left of it at first), crossing the centre of the first field. Corn had been grown in this in 1991, and the stubble had been burnt before we did this walk; there was no clear sign that the path had been reinstated after ploughing. Cross the rather brambly stile just left of a small oak, and then walk beside the hedge on the right. Where the hedge curves right, continue towards the church, down into a small valley, where you cross a bridge and stile and walk on in the same line, with the hedge on your left now. At the road, **either** turn left to continue the full medium-length walk: turn left again into Lewman Road, ignore all side turnings and at the T-junction (College Close) turn right. This soon brings you to the main road (A390), where you cross with great care and go a few yards right. Now pick up the directions soon after the

PROBUS CHURCH

The church's dedication to Saints Probus and Grace has given rise to much speculation. Several Continental saints were honoured with the title "Probus", meaning "the Good". Perhaps, however, this particular Probus came from Dorset: there was once a chapel called Lanprobi near Sherborne. "Grace was not a Saint," states Meyrick in his *A Pilgrim's Guide to the Holy Wells of Cornwall,* and he suggests that a misunderstanding of the Latin phrase "gratia et probus" (grace and goodness) may have led to her (or his?) appearance here in Cornwall. An English translation of the prayer containing the phrase is written on the Nave Screen. It appears that there was a Celtic monastery on this site from about the 6th century, and in the 10th century it was refounded along Saxon lines as a collegiate church with five Canons. The complex history of this establishment until it was appropriated by the Crown under the Chantry Act of 1545 is outlined by Charles Henderson in his notes on Probus. In 1612 James I sold off "all those prebends of St Probus in Cornwall with their houses, lands, barns, gardens, rents, tithes and other fruits", and they eventually became part of the Trewithen estate.

Much of the church was built about 1450 in the Perpendicular style, but the famous and graceful tower, with its delicate, almost lace-like carving, was the work of the following century. According to Arthur Mee it "has been described as one of the eight best towers in England." At almost 126 feet (38.35m.) it is the tallest medieval church tower in Cornwall. There are forty pinnacles (eight clusters of five), and the rich carving includes figures, plants and animals. According to Polsue in *Lake's Parochial History* it is built of "S. Stephens porcelain stone", a form of granite which is partially kaolinised and therefore somewhat easier to carve. Walk 2 includes a good deal of information about china stone in St Stephen parish; the stone for Probus, however, was quarried just north of the church at "the tenement of Gweal Martin or St Martin's Meadow" (Henderson), so Polsue's statement may be inaccurate. Like most Cornish churches, Probus was heavily "restored" by the Victorians, but the interior remains noble and still has many details from the ancient building, notably several memorials and the Tudor bench ends which were incorporated in the new Nave Screen. The church also has splendid acoustics, as we know after attending several of the concerts put on there each August as part of the Tregye Festival.

WALK 1

start of point 5, turning left at The Green. **Or**, to return directly to the church, turn right; follow this road round the left-hand corner and then turn right along Gwell-an-Nans. This new road is shown on the OS map as a footpath, and its name ("open field in the valley") reflects its rural recent past. Shortly after passing Hicks Close, take the path up on the left, passing the village hall before reaching the main road. Notice the rather sad relics of the old footpath at the top, including a fine stile, now totally redundant. Turn right for the church - and the pub.

FOR THE WALK ON THE NORTH SIDE OF THE VILLAGE, start by walking west along the main road, past the Lamplighter Restaurant and the Hawkins Arms. There are many attractive cottages, but the traffic must be very trying for those who live in them. Cross the road when you can.

5 Soon after passing Treviglas Rise (on the left), turn right along the little side-road marked "The Green", and then after a few yards right again. Now you are on a country path, and almost at once you have to cross a stile on your left - a muddy spot here, even in comparatively dry weather. Keep beside the hedge on your right, down to a footbridge, then uphill in the same line beyond that. Here, and also on the other side of the house ahead, there were many newly-planted trees. The beautiful house and its farm are called Lamellyn, meaning "Mill in the valley" - referring, obviously, to Probus Mill nearby, since the farm buildings are on a hill with a fine outlook to the west. (The two small boys who live at Lamellyn clearly take the adage about every Englishman's home's being a castle literally: one of them shot us dead with his gun, and the house's main entrance, on the far side, was formidably defended with plywood battlements.)

6 At Lamellyn you could turn right, passing beside the back of the house and following the main entrance drive (a public bridleway) to the road, where you pick up the directions at point 8; but a pleasant alternative is to walk down to Probus Mill first, even though there is little or nothing left of the original mill. For that, keep straight on past the main farm buildings and go through the gap on the left of the big shed with a corrugated roof. The path goes downhill; at first keep by the hedge on your left, but where that curves left continue ahead among the young trees towards the house below. On the other side of the valley runs the main London - Penzance railway line. Keep the hedge on your left as you approach the bottom of the slope, where there are a few steps down to a minor road. Turn left on that to look at the site of the watermill. Perhaps you will be able to work out where the millstream ran and where the waterwheel was - or perhaps you know, in which case I'd be glad if you told me. If you want to explore further, the right of way continues across the stream and railway and up through Cuskayne Farm to the A39.

7 To return to Probus you could simply retrace your steps up the minor road and continue along it for about half a mile; but we found that rather boring because of the high banks on both sides, so I would recommend returning to Lamellyn by the same path, turning left beside the house, as described at the start of section 6.

8 Turn right on the road at the end of the drive (or of the minor road from Probus Mill), and soon you are back among the houses of Probus, with the school on your right, and on the left a former Methodist Church, which, we were told, was shut down about 25 years ago. It is now a store selling second-hand furniture and other items, and glories in the name "Junk and Disorderly". Inside, many features of its days as a chapel remain, including the gallery running all around.

Before you leave Probus you might care to consider a visit to the County Demonstration Gardens, a unique 7.5-acre site which since its opening in 1972 has developed a wide range of displays designed to help people make their own gardens more attractive and productive. Other features include a Demonstration Apiary; a 20m.-long map of Cornwall showing examples of the different types of rock to be found; collections of wild flowers and poisonous plants; a Historical Garden; and a permanent exhibition, "Sculpture in the Garden Landscape". The Gardens are open every day from May to September (10 am to 5 pm); from October to April the opening hours are 10.30 to 4.30, Monday to Friday only. The Gardens are on the main road, about a quarter of a mile east of the church: within easy walking distance, but in view of the traffic you may well prefer to drive there.

Journey's end: the garden at the Hawkins Arms

WALK 2
ST STEPHEN-IN-BRANNEL, COOMBE, RESUGGA CASTLE AND TOLGARRICK
with a possible extension to GRAMPOUND
A choice of routes ranging from about 5 to 10 miles

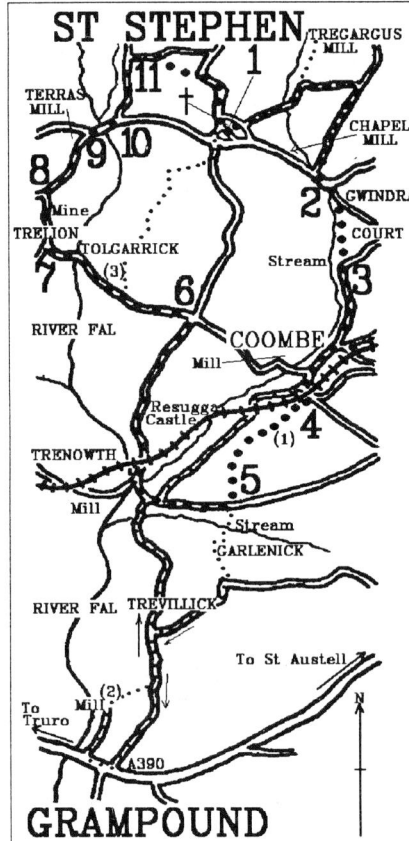

Of the walks in this book, this one has easily the greatest industrial archaeology interest, featuring mines, railways and especially china-stone grinding mills. It therefore might seem to belong more naturally to Around St Austell, and indeed Coombe is also included on a walk in that book. On the other hand, this walk links with the next one, because both follow the course of the River Fal, and Resugga Castle is part of the same system of Iron Age settlements and fortifications as Carvossa and Golden Fort. The walk includes a fine medieval church, a museum of motoring and much attractive countryside, with many old bridges and former watermills. The area is not much frequented by walkers, it would seem, and we did meet problems, notably at the points marked (1), (2) and (3) on the map, so before you set off I suggest you check my comments about these in the directions. Some sections of path are likely to be muddy. Much of the route is on roads - quiet ones, apart from a few yards along the A3058. There are pubs and shops at St Stephen and Grampound and a small shop at Coombe. If you like to take your own picnic food with you, Resugga Castle would make a pleasant spot to eat it: picnic tables are provided, the views are good, and it's a real suntrap on warm days. It has a car park, and would therefore make a good alternative point to start and end.

The directions start at St Stephen church (*). There is a car park by the recreation ground near the churchyard. Two pubs, the King's Arms and the Queen's Head, are near the church, and both are well-recommended for their food. I can personally vouch for the pasties at the King's Arms: genuinely "home-made", and even the "small" ones are a good plateful. We haven't used the Queen's Head, but I hope soon to investigate David Guthrie's remark in *Cornish Pubs:* "The pickled bums are remarkable and stimulate conversation." They are not, I presume, on the menu.

ST STEPHEN-IN-BRANNEL

The name of the local manor (sometimes found in other forms: Burnel, Brenel, Branel, Branwell ...)is added in order to distinguish this parish from two others in Cornwall, although in fact they are both called "St Stephens": one at Launceston, the other near Saltash. "The name Brannel is thought to mean corn ground," says *The Cornwall Village Book,* but Oliver Padel says it is "unexplained". St Stephen-in-Brannel has an attractive nucleus of granite and slate terraced houses with two pubs and an old school building clustered around its fine medieval church. As a market village it has a long history (and a colourful one: the sale of a wife for 4d at St Stephen market in 1835 recalls the opening of Hardy's *The Mayor of Casterbridge,* and the fictitious wife-sale happened at about the same date); but its growth to the status of a small town (population now about 2,000) began with William Cookworthy's discovery in about 1750 "that in the neighbourhood of the parish of St Stephens, in Cornwall, there are immense quantities of both the petuntse stone & the caulin". "Petuntse" and "caulin" (kaolin) were his versions of Chinese words; the English equivalents are "china stone" and "china clay". The landscape to the north is now dominated by great china-clay works; in contrast, the china-stone industry has declined, but relics of it still exist within and all around St Stephen, even on the southern side, which at first sight seems utterly rural. (For futher details, see the note on Terras Mill.) Before Cookworthy's time, in fact, such industry as there was in St Stephen parish consisted mainly of tin streaming in this area south of the village; there were also a few small metal mines one or two of which became quite important during the 19th century and continued working into the 20th. The brothers Silas and Joseph Hocking were sons of the owner of one of these mines; both were ordained Methodist ministers, and between the 1890s and the 1930s both became famous as the authors of literally scores of "healthy" novels carrying the Methodist message. Silas in particular achieved best-seller status, and Arthur Mee claims that he was the first writer ever to sell a million copies of his books in his lifetime. Now the Hockings are almost forgotten, but a nephew of theirs whose sales have been minute by comparison, the blind and almost deaf poet Jack Clemo, whose home used to be at nearby Goonamarris, has achieved a literary reputation that will surely last. His novel *Wilding Graft* gives a vivid and completely unglamourised picture of life in and around St Stephen (and also in Truro) during the late 1930s and early '40s. St Stephen's claim to a share in the glory of the Brontë sisters is a little more tentative: their mother was Cornish, and her surname, Branwell, suggests that her forebears hailed from this parish. In the world of sport St Stephen men have made a name for themselves in Cornish wrestling and especially tug-o'-war (the Terras team of 1914-37 was particularly celebrated, according to a newspaper article John Yeo showed me). Finally I must mention the achievement of a miner at the Victoria Inn, St Stephen, reported in *The West Briton* in 1844, who "ate half a pound of candles for a wager of a quart of beer. This done, he offered to eat another half pound for a further two quarts." (D.B.Barton: *Essays in Cornish Mining History, Volume 1)*

ST STEPHEN CHURCH

Although it lacks the beautiful carving of Probus and St Austell churches, St Stephen's does not lag far behind them in terms of generous size and pleasing proportions. The church lies in a hollow, but its tall tower commands a fine view. (Incidentally, Dr John Penderill-Church's book about William Cookworthy tells - perhaps with a grain or two of poetic licence - how he climbed the tower to survey the scene in his search for china clay, and thus found his way to Carloggas, about a mile to the north-east, where a small tin mine had created a white scar .... From that discovery flowed many changes for the people of this parish.) As mentioned elsewhere, there is some evidence that an earlier church was sited further east, but the existing building dates at least from Norman times: the larger font at the west end is said to bear carved portraits of William the Conqueror and his queen, along with what John Betjeman calls "Tiger Tim". The south door, with its unusual "nail-head" ornamentation, is the other notable remnant of the Norman church. Most of the building, including the tower, is the work of the 15th century. When the church was restored in 1854 it was less drastically Victorianised than many in the county. Much of the early woodwork has gone, but the wagon roof in the north aisle is original, and old carved pew-ends were used in constructing the pulpit. Under the floor of the Lady Chapel is the vault in which the Tanner family, Lords of the Manor of Brannel, were buried. The story is often told of how, when the vault was opened at the time of the restoration, the coffins were found to be unusually large - some over seven feet long. According to the church guide leaflet, descendants of the Tanner family on a visit from New Zealand in 1960 remarked that their own 13-year-old son was already over six feet tall; and the anonymous author of the piece about St Stephen in the WI's *The Cornwall Village Book* (1991) says that the present occupants of the manor-house site (Court Farm) are also exceptionally tall. One stained glass window at the east end of the church depicts china-clay working. The churchyard has a small Cornish cross, brought here from a field at Treneague Farm. The church guide suggests it may date from about the year 200, although Arthur Langdon in his book on Cornish crosses argues that no Christian cross in Cornwall is earlier than 5th century. Near the cross is a pillar sometimes called the "Reading Stone" or the "Crying Stone", because it is said that in the days before newspapers the latest news was announced here after Sunday morning services.

1 From the main church gate, opposite the King's Head, walk through the churchyard, continuing ahead past the church to the gate at the far end. Turn right at the road, then left at Trevear Road. Soon you cross the bridge over a stream which will accompany you on much of the first half of the walk.

Where the road bends quite sharply right, a track on the left beside houses gives access to a beautiful wooded valley and the ruined china-stone grinding mills of Tregargus and Trevear. Despite the neglect these have suffered since they fell out of use in the 1960s, they are still a fascinating and impressive monument to this once-important industry (some details of which are given later, especially in the note on Terras Mill), and the imaginative use that was made of water power calls to mind such places as Kennall Vale and the Luxulyan Valley. One big waterwheel was saved from destruction, but is now in an advanced state of decay. A brief description of Tregargus Mill, with two photographs, is in Industrial Archaeology of Cornwall *by A.C.Todd and Peter Laws (1972). In Alan M. Kent's novel,* Clay *(Amigo Books, 1991), Ben brings his girlfriend Chloe to this place. "She loved it down there," Ben remarks; but he "did not tell her that a man was killed here once under the weight of the massive grindstones. It would have ruined the picture for her, taken away the romance of the mill." From what I have been told locally, the "man" was little more than a boy, who, like many others, enjoyed taking rides on the merrygoround..... There is no public right of way in the valley: the site is still a registered quarry owned by English China Clays International and part of it is leased to the Goonvean and Rostowrack China Clay Company, which uses the old quarry pit above the mills for dumping. ECCI will probably grant permission to organised groups wishing to visit Tregargus (or Chapel Mill, mentioned later), but not to individuals.*

Continue along the road past Trevear (or Treveor) Farm - notice the mullioned windows of the farmhouse - and at the T-junction turn right. After about half a mile you reach the main road, A3058. Cross with care and turn left; luckily you don't have to brave the traffic for many yards.

2 Where the main road curves left, take the right turning, signposted Langerth and St Stephen's Coombe, and then cross the stile immediately on your right. The path now keeps fairly close to the stream on your right and takes you down this attractive valley. It is historically interesting for several reasons. Tin-streaming was carried out here: in 1780 streamers found two pieces of worked gold which may have been prehistoric, together with coins from the reigns of Edward III and Henry II. Shaft-mining also took place nearby, and the OS map marks an adit (drainage shaft) emptying into the stream from the high ground to the west. The mine, which seems to have produced little if any metal, was called Gwendra or Gwindra, which is the name of the farm on your left, now the site of a small industrial estate; but another name for the mine was Egloshellen, from another nearby farm, nowadays usually spelt "Eggloshellans". *Eglos* is a Cornish word for "church", so it seems probable that the original Celtic church was in this valley. A Cornish derivation of "hellen" seems possible: *hen-lann,* old cemetery; but Oliver Padel agrees with the church guide in suggesting a dedication to an unknown Celtic saint. Certainly the chief manor of the parish was here, the Manor of Brannel, which was probably the Domesday Manor called Burnel. Up on the left after you have passed through a kissing gate is Court Farm, which occupies the site of Court, the manor house, records of which go back at least to the 13th century. Its last occupants were the Tanner family, about whom there is a comment in the note about the church. The manor house is said to have been destroyed during the Civil

WALK 2

War. (Brannel, further south, was the manor farm.) In the distance ahead on the skyline is the stack of Ventonwyn Mine (the engine house is less clearly visible from this angle). The valley path ends rather muddily at a stile, beyond which is the entrance to Bodinnick Farm, and then comes the road.

3 Turn right there, still with the stream on your right; the wooded ground on the left is the site of old quarries. Soon you are entering Coombe village. The name of the first house shows that the stream has, or at any rate used to have, the same nickname as so many others near St Austell: the White River. Its official name is, I gather, the St Stephen River, though I have also heard it called the Wheal Arthur River, at least in its upper reaches near the old mica works of that name. The decrepit little waterwheel beside the house is another reminder of times past: Mr Jack Goldsworthy tells me that to his knowledge at least 27 waterwheels were powered by this stream alone. Continue past the playing fields and through the village - a peaceful spot in a pretty setting, though it seems a pity that so many characterless modern dwellings have been allowed to crowd around the original buildings such as the "Old Sunday School Cottage". Ignore the right turning, to St Stephen and Newquay (although you might care to go a little way up there to see the remains of Coombe Vale Mill on the right - another china stone mill); go left at the post office, and under the railway bridge.

4 Turn right immediately, following the footpath sign. The path runs beside the main London-Penzance line at first and then curves left, uphill. Soon another path crosses it, and here is the first of the "problems" I mentioned in the introductory note, marked (1) on the map. Officially the right of way continues straight ahead, but the fence ahead is securely barbed-wired. I have spoken about this both to the farmer and also to the Technical Officer of Restormel Borough, and I hope that before long a stile or some other way over or through will be provided; but at present the best solution seems to be to go a few yards right, where just to the left of an old gate the wire is fairly loose and relatively easy to negotiate. *(If, however, you find you cannot manage it, an alternative route using a minor road is available, as shown on the map. Return past the shop and turn left. After nearly a mile, at the T-junction turn right, and pick up the directions at line 7 in section 5.)* After the barbed wire, the next difficulty is to find the correct line of the path, because the old field-boundaries have gone. As far as I can tell, the proper route involves continuing uphill for a few yards on the line of the path by which you came, and then going diagonally right to the top of a small wooded or scrubby patch, where there are several clear paths running parallel. From here you get a good open view dominated by the huge waste tips of the Blackpool china-clay works; and then ahead you see the main line curving below in quite a deep valley. The hill on the far side of that is crowned with a circular field: this is Resugga Castle, details of which are given in a later note. From this vantage point it is particularly easy to appreciate how strategically placed the fortification was. Go through the metal farm gate on your left. The course of the path as shown on the OS maps is still not easy to relate to the modern field-pattern, but the farmer suggested walkers should keep by the hedge on the right at first, and then after the wooden farm gate curve left to the concrete reservoir marked "DAVEY", where there is another wooden gate. Now go down the tractor track, which soon brings you to a road. The big house ahead is Garlenick.

5 Turn right at the road, *but if you want to extend the walk to Grampound, fork left immediately, taking the track to Garlenick. Directions are given at the end of the main walk. Please note that "problem path (2)" is in this section.* For the more direct way back to St Stephen, continue along this pleasant, quiet, wooded road, which passes Treway farm (shown as "Mill" on early OS maps) and descends gradually to the valley of the River Fal. Ignore the first right and left turnings, but turn right after crossing a bridge (over the St Stephen River), following the sign to St Stephen. *First, however, I recommend a short diversion: cross the second bridge, a two-arched one, which takes you over the Fal, and continue along the road. After yet another bridge you come to a nicely modernised former corn mill which till recently was in use as a pottery. On the left nearby, still fairly complete but now mostly hidden among trees, are the remains of Trenowth China-Stone Mill. Return the same way.* The road to St Stephen takes you past the beautifully-situated Crow Hill Cottage with an old dry opposite (which dried the stone ground at the Coombe Vale Mill), under the viaduct and then quite steeply up Crow Hill. This is another area of historical interest. Habitation in ancient times is suggested by the discovery by tin-streamers nearby of an ornamental brass/bronze collar dating from about 100 AD. The viaduct, known officially as the Fal Viaduct, was rebuilt in 1884. Only one "stump" seems to remain of Brunel's original viaduct, which like all 41 other viaducts on his Cornwall Railway had a wooden super-structure. For some details about the old "fan viaducts" and their replacement, see the note about the Gover Viaduct in *Around St Austell* (Walk 3). The filled-in brick arch on

Crow Hill cottage and the Fal Viaduct

the right as you pass under the Fal Viaduct may be another relic of the original structure. The rough ground on both sides of the road was mined, mainly for lead, silver and iron: H.G.Dines gives details of Crowhill and New Crowhill Mines, which worked at various times between 1853 and 1913. Up on the right are what Barry Atkinson describes as "a very smally-constructed engine house, the stump of a stack and a burrow" (waste tip); unfortunately, he adds that they are "best viewed from the Trenowth railway viaduct", so watch out for them when you next cross that! The engine house was built for a 12-inch all-enclosed beam engine (like the one at Levant, currently being restored by the National Trust and the Trevithick Society), used for winding; the pumping was done by waterwheel. The OS map indicates an adit opening in the valley-bottom. This mine is supposed to have produced some uranium (see the later note on South Terras Mine); I have heard it said that people exploring the adit(s) have noticed a green luminosity there, but this probably comes from a type of moss rather than radioactivity, which is (perhaps unfortunately) invisible. Among the woods on the far side of the Fal is Trenowth. Like most of the many other places in Cornwall called "new farm", this one is very old: the manor of "Trefneweth" was given by King Edgar to one of his thegns in 969. Several chapels at Trenowth were licensed for worship in the 15th century, and the ruins of one of them were "still clearly visible" when Henderson was writing, probably during the 1920s: the Pathfinder map indicates "Chapel" among the trees beside the Fal. Trenowth House itself, I believe, dates only from the 1930s. At or near the top of the hill, turn right where signposted to explore Resugga Castle (*). Continue along the road as before. The long, low modern

RESUGGA CASTLE

The name derives from the Cornish *ros-googoo,* "hill-spur of the cave or hollow". Just where the cave or hollow is or was I don't know: possibly nearer to Resugga Farm, about a mile to the north. Like Carvossa and Golden Fort (both a short way south, and both visited on Walk 3), Resugga Castle is a Celtic Iron Age hill fort, and the closeness of all three to the Fal suggests the strategic and commercial importance of the river during the four or five centuries before Christ. Resugga's site, on a spur above the confluence of the St Stephen River and the Fal, is clearly ideal for guarding trade routes and sources of stream tin. The main enclosure, surrounded by a rampart about nine feet high and a ditch about three feet deep, is D-shaped and about 120 yards across at its widest point. On the right side of the car park as you face the earthwork is a sunken entrance trackway which passes between two outlying ramparts; these may be relics of an annexe to the main fort, possibly for the corralling of cattle. Recently Restormel Borough Council, in conjunction with the late-lamented Manpower Services Commission, improved the facilities for visitors here and provided a useful explanatory notice; I hope this will survive the attentions of the weather and/or vandals longer than some of the picnic tables have. Incidentally, the 19th-century OS maps indicate another, smaller, earthwork named Burghgear, "the house of the fort or round", a short way to the south (surprisingly, not on the main spur opposite Resugga but on the slope south of Treway farm). There is no trace of it on the modern maps.

WALK 2

building ahead, on the edge of St Stephen, is Brannel School (comprehensive); on the skyline are good examples of both types of china-clay sand tips, the conical "sky-tips" and the "finger-tipping" which, being much safer and more practical for large volumes of sand, has now superseded it. The tips you can see ahead are at the Melbur, Virginia, Treviscoe, Goonvean and Trethosa works, and Blackpool is to the right.

6 At the crossroads, for the shortest way back to St Stephen continue ahead; but for the full recommended route, turn left, following the sign to Trelion (pronounced as per the animal's name, and sometimes spelt "Trelyon"). Before long this road descends to the Fal valley at Tolgarrick Mill. *There is a footpath to St Stephen from Tolgarrick. Using it would shorten the walk and avoid some road walking; on the other hand it would mean missing what I feel are some of the most interesting details. At present this path constitutes "problem No. (3)", because the first part of it, as shown on the OS maps, has become blocked. I understand from the Technical Officer at Restormel that the path is likely to be re-routed using the drive to Tolgarrick Farm; I have shown the proposed route on my map. If and when this change becomes official there will presumably be signs indicating the new route. Should you decide to go that way, turn right just before Tolgarrick farmhouse (the owners have put up signs), then go to the metal gate in the hedge on the left, close to the house. Cross that and the small stile just beyond, and then go diagonally across the field to a small gate, which is down by a stream and so not visible from a distance. After crossing the bridge, walk by the hedge on the right. From here you have a view to the left of a converted engine house, part of South Terras Mine: see the full walk for details. Cut across the corner of the field to keep left of Resugga Farm buildings. The pond is marked on the maps as a reservoir. After the kissing gate, go straight on along the lane, passing the comprehensive school, beside which stands the old Rectory, a grey house in the neo-classical style. Take the footpath on the right, signed Rectory Road, which runs through a new housing estate. Keep more-or-less straight on, crossing a patch of waste ground not yet built on in December 1991, through another kissing gate, and turn left at the road. Cross Gwindra Road and continue along Fore Street to the church.* For the full walk, continue down to Tolgarrick Mill (presumably a corn mill, but little if anything seems to have survived in recognisable form). From the bridge over the Fal can be seen an old stack, a few yards up-river, and beside it are the overgrown ruins of a mine's treatment plant. This is a relic of the most important mine in this area, South Terras (*). Continue along the road.

7 At the T-junction turn right. This hamlet, consisting of little more than a few cottages, some of which have now been merged and christened "Tinners House", is called Trelion, meaning "farmstead of the flat stones".

8 At the next T-junction again turn right, and soon you reach a converted engine house, now called "Stack House". The rotative beam engine which it had held stopped working about 1906, and even before it was removed for

SOUTH TERRAS MINE

The first recorded output of South Terras dates from 1873, but how much earlier than that work started is not known. It began as an iron mine, producing also a little ochre and tin; along with these the miners found a mysterious mineral (actually torbernite) which they nicknamed "Green Jim". ("Jim" was a reference to James Harris-James, the mine's managing director/agent.) In the early years this was hand-picked, packed in barrels and exported to Germany for use as a pigment in glass and black porcelain. In 1889 J.H.Collins was asked to inspect the mine, and the contents of his report were, as he puts it in his *Observations on the West of England Mining Region* (1912), "boomed in the newspapers throughout Europe and the United States for all they were worth, and more." "This lode," he says in the same book, "is certainly one of the most important deposits of uranium ores yet discovered anywhere in the world." And in a footnote he adds, "I say nothing of its radium content, as I have no special information thereon; but it has been stated that contracts have been made for the supply of radium in large quantities." Radium was discovered by the Curies in 1898. It is often said that Mme Curie visited South Terras as a possible source of radium for medical purposes, but there is no evidence for this belief, and Courtenay Smale (who has made a close study of the mine's history) is very sceptical about the story. What can be established is that Mme Curie's Preparator carried out sampling at the mine in 1912. At about that time the French Société Industrielle du Radium took over the mine, but the war put a stop to its work. A radium-extraction factory which was set up after the war closed in 1929. H.G.Dines's account of the mine ends, "Attempts were made to sell the tailings as radioactive manure." In the good old academic tradition, he resists any temptation to add an exclamation mark. The Cornwall Heritage Project's booklet, *China Clay District Driveabout*, points out that another radioactive element discovered by Mme Curie, polonium, was also produced at South Terras, and that "weight for weight it is a hundred thousand million times more toxic than cyanide gas." (Polonium and actinium cake was, Mr Smale tells me, sent to the Continent, mixed with glycerine and used as a relief from rheumatism.) The miners worked only during the summer because so much water entered the workings at other times; even so, I wonder about the life expectancy of the men who ate their crowst amidst the Green Jim and grew the spuds and turnips in their pasties with the aid of that manure ....

use at a china-clay pit the building had been bought for domestic conversion: "a possibly unique instance," Kenneth Brown tells me, "where the roof, door and window joinery were retained for the dwelling and did not accompany the engine to its new home." The engine house was built by a small enterprise called Terras Mine. Now the road descends gradually, with the pleasant countryside of the Fal valley to your right. The ground on both sides was worked by Terras Mine for tin during the 1870s and '80s, mainly by means of open cuts.

9 At the main road (A3058) turn right - but first have a look at the big old building on your left, rather patched and dilapidated and partly adapted for use as a greengrocer's-cum-florist's shop, but still of considerable historical interest. This is Terras Mill (*). To continue the walk, procede with care a short way along the main road, crossing the Fal at Terras Bridge. "Terras" may mean "three fords", and a glance at the OS map shows that there could well have been as many as that at this point in the valley.

TERRAS MILL AND THE CHINA-STONE INDUSTRY

St Stephen china stone, a partially-decomposed form of granite, has long been recognised as a useful building material. Charles Thurlow tells me he has noticed at least 35 references in *Lake's Parochial History* (c.1870) to the use of "St Stephen granite" for carved features inside churches. Probus church tower is probably built of it (see Walk 1), as well as the one at St Stephen itself; so too is the tower at St Columb Major, and William Cookworthy's discovery of this fact in 1748 was one reason why he turned to the St Stephen area in his search for good-quality materials for the manufacture of ceramics. With the rapid growth of the china-clay industry from the late 18th century onwards increasing quantities of the stone were quarried. Ground to a fine powder and mixed with china clay, it acts as a flux in the firing of porcelain, and (to quote William Cookworthy's patent of 1768) "gives the ware .... its transparence and mellowness." Several mills were built in and around St Stephen, employing waterwheels to drive grinding pans, the bases of which were made of china stone. A mixture of water and small lumps of the stone was fed in, and revolving arms propelled big blocks of china stone on top of it, creating a white "mud". John Yeo, the owner of Terras Mill, showed me where a leat once brought water from the River Fal; the wheelpit made for a waterwheel built at the Bartle Carn Brea Foundry in 1898; the low building housing the grinding pans; and the settling-tanks where the process of drying the "mud" began. All this is behind the big building with its rust-gaudy corrugated roof, now in use as a shop and store. Until about 1934 this was the mill's kiln or dry, built like a china-clay dry with linhay (storage area - pronounced "linny") alongside the drying pans: the remains of its stack can still be seen at the far end, and the fire grates were just to the right of the present shop as you enter. The building was used as stables for about ten years from 1945, and relics of this episode in its history are still clear to see. Terras Mill may not be among Cornwall's architectural gems, but I wholeheartedly support Mr Yeo in his determination to resist tempting offers from "developers" with plans to beautify it - or, more probably, replace it with yet another housing estate. As far as I know, no grinding of china stone is done in Cornwall now, and only one company continues to quarry it: suitable types of feldspar, which is the important constituent of china stone, can now be obtained more economically abroad, for example from Canada and Scandinavia.

The ruins of another china-stone mill in St Stephen are beside Hawkins Motors, on the A3058 a few hundred yards west of point 2 on the map. This was Chapel Mill, an interesting name because no-one remembers a chapel on this site, but Henderson notes that the area was named as "Chapel Park" (=field) as long ago as 1578. Although at first sight little besides the stack seems to have survived, Charles Thurlow and John Hawkins tell me that there are three grinding pans, a waterwheel, leats and other remains. The possibility of visits to this site by organised parties is mentioned in section 1.

WALK 2

10 Take the first left turning, which soon brings you to the "Automobilia" Motor Museum (*). Even if old cars don't interest you, you may well be glad of the chance to visit the museum's snack bar. Continue along the road as before. What appears to be a long, low hill on your left is in fact a waste tip for fine sand and mica residues from china-clay workings. The OS map describes the area as an "Experimental Seeding Ground", and evidently the experiment has been very successful. Some details about modern techniques of fertilising and seeding the steeper slopes of old tips are given in the Cornwall Heritage Project's booklet, *China Clay District Driveabout*.

11 Turn right. The road runs uphill through attractive, rolling countryside (mainly sheep-pasture, apparently), and soon brings you to Treneague Mill, (pronounced "Trenayg") with its attendant farm buildings and cottages. Treneague was once the site of an old chapel, and an ancient Cornish cross was found in one of its fields: see the note about St Stephen church. Take the signed footpath on the right (to Trethosa Road). The path leads you through three kissing gates (though the second has almost gone, and the third is much patched), and then around the new primary school. At the road turn right. This soon brings you down to St Stephen church.

Automobilia
Cornwall's Motor Museum

Mr Colin Vincent, who owns the Museum and has restored many of the old cars exhibited, has told me a little about the history of the building, which is still called The Old Mill. It was a working corn mill until World War II, and also housed a general store where almost everything imaginable could be bought and which even offered a tooth-pulling service. The corn grinding was done at the first floor level, and when the machinery was being dismantled someone decided that the obvious way to remove the millstones was simply to drop them out through a window or other opening. Instead of breaking up when it fell as expected, however, one stone landed on its edge and rolled down the main street. Apparently no-one was killed or injured, but the incident is vividly remembered locally. During the latter part of the war the Old Mill was used as a U.S. Army food store. Mr Vincent and his wife Carole launched the motoring museum about ten years ago, and now they have a collection of over fifty vehicles ranging in date from a 1904 Belsize to an E-type Jaguar of 1966, and in luxuriousness from a 1927 Austin Chummy to a magnificent 1931 Rolls Phantom 11 Continental; there are also vintage motorcycles and early commercial vehicles. Displays of "automobilia" include accessories, period signs and adverts, and you may want to search out a spare part for an elderly vehicle of your own among the "Autojumble" on the third floor. Opening hours are 10 - 4 in April, May and October, and 10 - 6 from June to September. A café and a children's play area are provided.

WALK 2

EXTENDING THE WALK TO INCLUDE GRAMPOUND

This makes an attractive addition, but the suggested return route includes near the start a neglected short section of footpath likely to be both boggy and overgrown. If you found this unusable you would need to retrace your footsteps most of the way back.

Starting at point 5 in the directions, take the track down to the mansion called Garlenick or Garlinnick. The full meaning of the name is not known, but Padel suggests the first syllable probably derives from Cornish *cor,* a hedge or boundary. He does not refer to the "ker" or "gear"(fort, round) shown on the old maps just to the west: see the end of the note about Resugga Castle. After crossing a stream - much frequented by ducks - the track curves right beside the house, looking rather like a cross between a Victorian school and a castle, then left past cottages and farm buildings. After a farm gate you are on the main entrance drive, passing through Garlenick Woods. At the road turn right, soon passing the restored former farmhouse of Nantellan. More attractive old farm buildings - and these still in use for farming - are on the right as you reach a T-junction; this is Trevillick. Turn left, and soon you pass Higher Trevillick. After that there are few buildings for half a mile or so till the road becomes Pepo Lane and descends into Grampound. It reaches the main road beside St Nun's Church, the market hall and the old cross-shaft: see the note on Grampound in Walk 3. Turn right, past the pub, and continue till you reach Mill Lane, on your right, which comes shortly before the River Fal bridge. Turn up this road. After several new houses, you will pass the surgery on your right, followed by small "cliffs" created by quarrying. The large old buildings ahead and to the left at the end of the road are or were Grampound Town Mills. This grist mill is described by D.E.Benney in *Cornish Watermills* (1972); he traces its history back to 1607 and remarks, "It is indeed a rarity to find a watermill three and a half centuries later still operational and prospering." At the time he was writing, one of its two waterwheels had recently been renovated, although electricity was by then powering the mill. Unfortunately, little if anything of the mill itself can be seen from the road, and whether it still operates I do not know. Follow the footpath sign (to Trevillick), which takes you under a building into what looks like part of the quarry. The path goes up quite steeply on the right: this is problem-patch (2). If it is too overgrown to be visible, the metal handrail should help you find it. It is likely to be very wet underfoot here. Soon the path becomes clearer, but probably even muddier. Beyond the small metal gate things improve. Ignore the obvious path up the field (keeping to the valley): go up to the top left corner, where there is a stile to the road by which you came down to Grampound earlier. Retrace your steps now till you reach the two Trevillick farms. There continue ahead, following the sign to St Stephen. Notice the small stone arch built into a barn wall at Trevillick, on the right beside the road. According to Charles Henderson's notes on Creed parish, it is inscribed "Found at St Naunter W.P.", referring to a chapel and holy well of St Naunter which once existed on the left side of the road about a quarter of a mile further along. The road runs through lush, rolling, wooded countryside with the River Fal down to the left and little besides the occasional farm vehicle on the road or train in the distance to break the silence. At the T-junction turn left, picking up the directions at line 7 of section 5.

WALK 3
TREGONY, CREED, GRAMPOUND, TREWITHEN AND GOLDEN

About 8 miles.
A walk of about 5 miles omitting Tregony is also suggested,
and another of about 4 miles covering Tregony and Golden.
A further possibility would be a 3-mile walk including only Grampound and Trewithen.

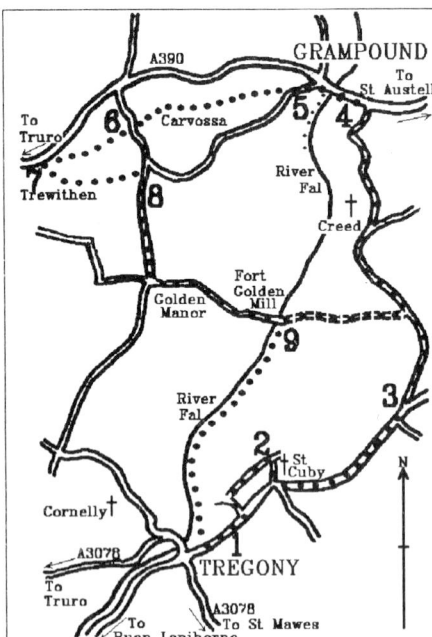

Despite nearly a mile on an A-road, this is a strong candidate as my favourite walk in Around Mevagissey: *not only is the countryside beautiful, but there is an exceptionally high level of historical interest, plus the opportunity (except on Sundays and from October to February) to visit one of Cornwall's great gardens. Most of the route is on minor roads or well-made tracks, so it would be a good choice during a wet spell; the only likely trouble-spots from that point of view would be on the path beside the River Fal. The terrain is quite hilly, but the walk is not strenuous. Shops, tearooms, restaurants and pubs are at Tregony and Grampound, and there are public toilets at Tregony.*

For the 8- and 4-mile walks I suggest Tregony as the starting point, because parking is comparatively easy there, and by beginning at Tregony you get the main-road walking out of the way quickly. For the 3- and 5-mile routes you will probably need to park on a side-road in Grampound; or if you are including a visit to the garden and/or house at Trewithen you may be able to leave your car there while you do a walk, provided that there is not too much pressure on the quite small car park.

1 Walk up the wide main street of Tregony (*), past the King's Arms and Tregony Methodist Chapel. Immediately beyond that, turn left (toilets here) and then right, opposite the entrance to Tregony Holiday Park. Notice the old pump. The little road lives up to its name of Back Lane by showing you the backs of the cottages and houses along the main street, and also of the primary school. Soon you come to Tregony Church (*).

2 Turn right, and then left along the main road. There is a pavement as far

TREGONY

Unusually, the name is stressed on the first syllable; a spelling of it from about 1540 is "Tregny". Polsue in *Lake's Parochial History* explains the name as "Tre-Cenia", "the castle on the Fal", since Cenia or Cenion appears to have been the Roman name for the river. Polsue's theory is no longer accepted ("farm of Rigni" is Padel's suggestion); neither is his statement that the Romans built a castle on the high ground overlooking the point where the stream on the south side of Tregony joins the river. A century or more after the Norman Conquest, however, the manors of Tregony became the property of a family called de la Pomerai (otherwise Pomeroy), and they built a house on that site which seems later to have developed into a castle. Under their influence the small community rapidly gained status. Tregony Bridge was built, thus effectively cutting off Grampound from navigation; a new parish was created, a new church (St James's) was built just above the bridge, and a Priory was established beside the castle in the 13th century. The right to hold fairs and markets was granted, and also, at certain periods, the right to be represented in Parliament. (In 1620, when it was Incorporated, Tregony became a "pot-waller" or "pot-walloper" borough with two MPs, in which the right to vote was given to householders with a hearth big enough to boil a pot of a certain size on. This was one of the abuses ended by the 1832 Reform Act.) Several profitable woollen mills operated in and around the village, and in 1631 Tregony had 36 alehouses. All this prosperity was, of course, dependent on the success of the port, and by the 16th century that was seriously threatened, mainly because of silt resulting from tin-streaming. Despite at least two dredgings of the river during Henry VIII's reign, the quays became unusable, and St James's Church was abandoned by 1538 because the river kept flooding the low-lying ground on which it was built. *Old Cornish Bridges* by Henderson and Coates (1928) has a fascinating account of abortive attempts late in the 17th century to make the Fal navigable again as far as Trenowth (north of Grampound - see Walk 2) by a system of sluices and locks. The decline of the river trade and of places like Tregony continued; indeed, one settlement called Sheepstall or Sheepstores, a mile below Tregony, once the site of a market, chapel and leper-house, disappeared completely. The building of Sett Bridge at Ruan Lanihorne in the 1880s marked the recognition that navigation on the upper reaches of the Fal was finished for ever, and then as more and more silt from the china-clay district flowed down the river, Ruan too became inaccessible to vessels of any size. (See Walks 6 and 7 in *Around the Fal.*) "The ugly white river of Fal discharges its burden of sand and gravel," wrote Henderson and Coates; compare the White River at Pentewan (Walk 6 in *Around St Austell*), which now, like the Fal, runs clear again. A walk round Tregony now reveals nothing of the castle, priory or St James's Church, and even the old bridge has been replaced; but the beautiful, wide main street hints at former glories, and there are interesting old buildings such as the two-storey almshouses known as The Gallery, dated 1696 but heavily restored about a century ago. They were originally described as "a hospital for decayed housekeepers".

TREGONY CHURCH

The Church of St Cuby the Abbot is the original mother-church. A Celtic church, little more than a wattle hut, was probably built on the site in the 5th or 6th century, and the earliest parts of the present building date from the 11th century. As explained in the note about Tregony, a new parish of Tregony was formed from part of Cuby in the 13th century, but less than 300 years later its church of St James was destroyed, and its congregation began walking up the hill again to the old place of worship. In 1828 and again in 1899 it was almost completely rebuilt, so that the south porch and the 14th-century tower are almost the only medieval work remaining, apart from the beautiful 12th-century font. There is, of course, a great deal more to see than I have mentioned, and I strongly recommend the church guide, which includes scholarly and fascinating accounts of the life of St Cuby and the history of Tregony.

as the Roseland School (comprehensive); after that you will need to walk on the right to face the oncoming traffic. I apologise for having to include main-road walking, which is never pleasant, but this is not usually very busy, and visibility is generally good. The entrance to Tregonhayne marks roughly the half-way point.

3 Soon after the right turning to Govelly, cross and turn left for Creed Church. This very minor road - little more than a lane - gives you, despite the high hedges, a good view ahead across the china-clay district, and at the top of the first slope a panorama on the left which includes glimpses of Creed church in the valley and the top of Probus church tower on the skyline to the left, beyond the woods of Trewithen. *A few yards past the right turning to Halbote and Bohago Farms, you could turn left on the grassy track and continue ahead to just below Golden Mill, returning to Tregony from there by taking the path on the left beside the Fal as described in point 9.* Continuing towards Grampound, the road descends to a pretty valley, crosses a small stream which I shall mention again later, and then comes Creed church (*), among nicely-restored old farm buildings. The River Fal is just below, and you can walk down to it if you like, keeping just left of the hedge or trees at the bottom of the graveyard. (The Trewithen Estate gamekeeper told us that there was once a bridge here or close by, and that the path continued up to Trewithen House, enabling the Johnstone family to walk to and from church; unfortunately it now stops dead at the river.) Something about the setting of Creed church reminds me of St Winnow, despite the fact that the Fal hides away so shyly here, in contrast to the wide sweep of the Fowey there; but

CREED CHURCH

Tybesta was one of the seventeen manors that made up the Cornish part of the Duchy of Cornwall when it was created in 1337, and Creed was its church. Its dedication is of special interest to my wife because she was born at Crediton, whose name apparently derives from the same female Irish saint, Credie. Most of the building dates from the 14th and 15th centuries, although there are a few small relics of the Norman structure. The restoration of this church, carried out in 1904 under the patronage of the "Squire" of Trewithen, was much less harsh than most 19th-century restorations - in fact, as Betjeman puts it, "It is refreshingly unrestored"; and I would add, almost as delightful inside as out. The typed sheet available in the church usefully lists nine interior features in particular to look for. Two I would especially pick out are the inclusion of leather tanning among the carvings on the table to the right of the altar (a tribute, presumably, to the tannery in Grampound), and the photograph and other details near the organ about the discovery in 1791 by a Rector of Creed of Titanium, originally called Manaccanite because the sample of sand in which it was found came from Manaccan, near Helford. Not mentioned in the list, but worth a look, is the Parish Bier, last used in 1963. A placard explains that three teams of six men used to share the work of bringing it and the coffin from Grampound.

perhaps in reality it's only peace and beauty that the two have in common. (And holiness? I'll leave others to judge that.) Back to the road, which now climbs out of the valley. At the top of the hill a right turning leads to Manheirs, one of several Cornish farms whose name refers to a prehistoric longstone: compare Tremenhere near Stithians, for example (*A Second View from Carn Marth,* Walk 8), where a menhir still stands. From here you have a view over Grampound, with Grampound Road on the skyline. Now the road widens. Notice on the right a wooden post with the base of a cross in front of it. Charles Henderson states that this is a relic of one of four crosses erected in this parish during the 15th century, perhaps to mark a place "where dead bodies are rested on the way to their burial - that prayers may be made and the bearers take some rest." As you enter Grampound you pass a former chapel of the Bible Christians, dated 1881, now converted into a private house. (For some details about the best-known of Cornish Bible Christians, Billy Bray, see Walks 1 and 4 in the book I have just referred to.)

4 At the main road in Grampound (*) turn left to continue the walk, but first it's worth turning right to look at the many interesting features of that end of the village, including St Nun's Church beside the small Guildhall and clock tower; then on the right the old Manor House, with the Manor Tannery (*) next door; and almost opposite that, The Hollies (*), the house just beyond the newsagents of the same name. Returning down the street now, if you call

Grampound

WALK 3

GRAMPOUND

Its name betrays its origin: the "great bridge" was built during the 13th century at what was then the lowest bridging-point on the Fal. A document of 1299 refers to the "Borough of Ponsmur", which is the Cornish equivalent. The bridge itself was apparently never very impressive, and the "grand" presumably indicates its importance to the main trade- and pilgrim-route through south Cornwall. The old bridge was demolished in 1834 and a new one built a few yards to the north to carry the new main road: see point 5 in the directions. Official status as an incorporated borough came in 1332 or 1333: this conferred some tax exemptions and the rights to hang thieves and to hold weekly markets. In the 16th century the right to send two MPs to Westminster was granted. Grampound became perhaps the most notorious of all the "Rotten Boroughs" when the buying of votes there was cited by Lord John Russell as a prime example of electoral corruption; as a result, Grampound ceased to be represented as early as 1821, whereas other Rotten Boroughs survived until the 1832 Reform Act. Because Creed church is so far away, there has been a Chapel of Ease in Grampound since at least 1370; it was dedicated at various times to St Mary, St Barnabas and St Naunter. After the borough was disenfranchised and lost its mayor and corporation the chapel fell into ruins; some of the old stonework, including a fine rose window, was acquired by Samuel Trist in 1827, and built into the entrance lodge of his new vicarage at Veryan a few years later. In 1869 a new chapel was built and dedicated to St Nun. St Nun or Non was the mother of St David of Wales, and her name also appears in that of Altarnun, on the edge of Bodmin Moor. The little Guildhall and clock tower, with the 15th-century Pentewan stone market cross in the street beside them, are a reminder of Tregony, and the comparison helps to highlight the urgent need for a bypass here. To me, in fact, it seems even more urgent than at Probus and Sticker, but it's not likely to come till 1999 at the earliest.

at the Dolphin Inn do have a good look at the wonderful old photograph of Grampound hanging over the fireplace. It was taken about 1900, and shows the children of the village lined up across the street, which sems to be surfaced with mud and has no traffic except one horse and cart; otherwise, little seems to have changed in nearly a century. (The same picture is in *Victorian and Edwardian Cornwall from Old Photographs* by John Betjeman and A.L.Rowse [Batsford, 1974]). Opposite the pub is the 17th-century Cottage Restaurant, where you could get light refreshments; a little further down the hill is a teashop (Perran House, on the right); and beyond that is Eastern Promise, a Chinese restaurant which attracts custom from far and wide: excellent if you want to give yourself a treat *after* the walk! Just past the junior school is the bridge over the Fal, an earlier version of which gave the village its name; but nowadays I suspect that most motorists and even some pedestrians cross it without noticing. *On the left immediately beyond the bridge is a footpath that runs beside the river for about a quarter of a mile; it would make a pleasant little diversion. There is some talk about*

GRAMPOUND MANOR TANNERY

This is Cornwall's last remaining tanyard for the making of heavy leather - and yet Grampound alone had at least five tanneries in the mid-19th century. An interesting article about it by Byron Edwards in the November 1991 issue of *Cornish Life* claims it to be "one of the only two oak bark outlets in Britain, possibly Europe". (The other British one is in Devon.) Much of historical interest remains at the Manor Tannery, but unfortunately it is not open to the public for visits, partly because of the dangers involved. A detailed account of its history and the processes employed, with many photographs, is *Oak Bark Tanning in Cornwall* by Mary Cowan Doxsee; this seems to me to deserve publication, but at present is available only at the Courteney Library of the Royal Institution of Cornwall, Truro. The tannery achieved some fame when its leather was used in the construction of Tim Severin's curragh, "Brendan", which sailed from Tralee in May 1976 and reached Boston more than a year later, tracing the route thought to have been taken by an early Irish saint. William Croggon is quoted in the *Cornish Life* article as saying, "We quite deliberately use traditional methods of tanning to produce very specialist leather. While everyone else is aiming to get cheaper and cheaper, we have found a niche in the market for really top class shoes. These shoes sell all over the world and some of the highest in the land have our leather under their feet." The Croggon family have been involved in tanning since 1712; *croghen,* by the way, is the Cornish word for "skin", but Mr Croggon assured me this is mere co-incidence: the family name was originally "Caroggon", and the Caroggons were farmers.

THE HOLLIES

This house, which belongs to the owners of the tannery, has an unusual garden of 1 - 2 acres, much of it set out in island beds. In recent years it has been opened to the public occasionally in aid of charity, and a visit would be a pleasant addition to your walk if you could time it to coincide. Details for the current season are given in the annual *Gardens of Cornwall Open Guide,* or you could enquire by telephoning 0726-882474.

the possibility of extending the path further south to Golden or west to Barteliver, but at present it's a "no through road".

5 Go a little further along the main road and take the left turning signed to Barteliver and Golden Mill. At once you are among attractive old cottages. Don't follow the road round to the left at Glenview, but keep straight on past more pretty cottages. The road soon becomes a track running almost due west along a ridge parallel with the valley where runs the A390, glimpses of which you may occasionally get. The track you are on is shown as the only road linking Grampound and Probus (and therefore St Austell and Truro) on the OS map of 1813; the new road was built in 1834, so the ancient ridgeway turnpike road was superseded at about the same time as the earliest tramways (railways for horse-drawn wagons) were being laid in Cornwall. Just how ancient it is can be deduced from the fact that it runs right beside an ancient earthwork, Carvossa (*). This is easily recognised by the clump of trees just after the turning to the farm of the same name - not quite, as you might expect, at the highest point on the ridgeway, which comes a little later, where a road crosses. The northern ditch and rampart are very obvious, on the left close to the track.

CARVOSSA

This Iron Age settlement was taken over by the Romans (it may be the trading settlement referred to by Ptolemy as Voliba). Excavations in 1968-70 produced evidence that between about 60 and 130 AD its population outgrew the original oblong enclosure, some of them setting up home in the outer ditch or beyond. The main entrance was on the east. In addition to the ridgeway that still skirts the northern edge of the earthwork, there was a road running south-east from it to the Fal. A possible meaning of the name is "bloody (or bleeding) castle"; that's something to set your imagination working!

---

6 At the road, EITHER turn left for the more direct way back to Tregony, picking up the directions at point 8; OR go straight on along the ridgeway, here signposted as a bridle path to Probus, if you want to visit Trewithen Gardens and/or House (see the boxed note for opening times). Where the main driveway curves left to Trewithen Farms, continue straight on. Soon you have a view of Trewithen House left; and finally the old road regains its original status by joining the modern A390.

7 Here turn left along the main drive to Trewithen (*). Following a visit to

---

TREWITHEN

The name refers to the woods surrounding the mansion (Cornish *gwyth*, trees), which is basically 17th-century, but was greatly improved after 1715 when the estate was bought by the Hawkins family. Trewithen has a double link with Walk 6 in *Around St Austell:* firstly because the house is constructed largely of Pentewan stone, and secondly because the Hawkins family was responsible for building Pentewan harbour and railway. The grounds at Trewithen were much improved by Thomas Hawkins ("Squire" from 1738 to 1766) and some of his successors, but the beauty of the garden was created largely by George Horace Johnstone, who inherited the estate in 1904. If you would like to know the history of the house, the garden and their owners in more detail, see the excellent video film which is shown every hour on the hour during the garden's opening times: every day except Sundays from 1st April to 30th September, from 10am to 4.30pm. Dogs must be on leads. The house is open to visitors from April to July on Monday and Tuesday afternoons, 2 - 4.30pm. (These details are correct for 1991; to check for the current year, see the *Gardens of Cornwall Open Guide.*)

the gardens, continue in the same direction past the house and a small lake; ignore the left turning (to the nurseries), and go on through the park to the road, where you turn right for Golden and Tregony *(or left and then immediately right to return to Grampound via Barteliver, completing the 3-mile walk).*

GOLDEN MANOR

Although the name seems appropriate for this charmed spot, it is in fact thought to be a corruption of the name of the family that owned it until 1514, the Wolvedons. In that year it became the property, through marriage, of the Tregion family (pronounced "Trudgeon"). 63 years later, disaster came upon them when Francis Tregion was found to be sheltering a young Roman Catholic priest, Cuthbert Mayne. The latter was hanged, drawn and quartered at Launceston, and one of the "quarters" was put on display at Tregony. His head decorated the gate at Launceston Castle for a while, and part of the skull was preserved at Lanherne (see Walk 2 in *Around Newquay)* as a holy relic. Eventually, in 1974, Cuthbert Mayne was canonised by the RC Church. Tregian forfeited his estates and spent 24 years in prison. Finally he was released - by personal order of Queen Elizabeth, according to Norden - but had to live within five miles of the Fleet Prison. At last he was permitted to leave the country, and he died in 1608 at a Jesuit house in Lisbon. Tonkin states that in later years local people would show visitors the place where the priest was hidden, "under an old tower". The most intriguing building is the ancient cowshed on the left, which has a sundial and most of the external features you would expect of a medieval chapel, and "Chapel" is what the OS map labels it. Others with equal firmness call it "a medieval hall building". Inside there is a spiral staircase. Charles Henderson writes interestingly about this barn in his notes on Probus parish, concluding that it was "probably the mediaeval house itself", and is likely to have had an oratory on the upper floor. The special magic of Golden is perhaps created by the contrast between its violent past and the utter tranquillity of its present. In fact, I don't think I have ever seen another human being there, and even the farm animals seem unusually silent and placid!

GOLDEN FORT

This hill fort, often referred to as "The Warren", is in many ways similar to Carvossa, though it is larger, slightly different in plan, and had its entrance to the north-west. Like Carvossa it was taken over by the Romans and was conveniently situated at or near the tidal limit of an important trading river. Golden is another fort often held to be Ptolemy's Voliba. There are in fact six possible candidates in the Grampound area, and it could even be that all of them together made up the trading settlement given that name. Some scholars have suggested that "Vol" is an early version of "Fal", but that theory appears to be undermined by the fact, mentioned in the note on Tregony, that the river seems to have been called the Cenion in Roman times.

The barn at Golden

8 Continue south along this pleasant country road and take the left turning signposted to Golden Mill. Almost at once you come to Golden Manor (*), on the right, with the farm buildings opposite. Roughly where the road bends right is the site of Golden Well, described by Meyrick as Holy and "an ancient stone structure in need of attention". Although very close to the road (on the right) it is not visible from it, and it stands on private land. So too does Golden Fort (*), on the hill to the left, and you would need permission from the Trewithen estate to go up the path to it. There is no need to feel too frustrated, because the road down to the Fal is delightful enough in itself. The farm buildings near the bottom of the hill are called Golden Mill. There's no sign of a waterwheel now, but a legal document dated 1637 refers to "both mills at Golden". Golden Mill was certainly working by early Tudor times, because a bond was lodged during Henry VIII's reign for the building of a weir to improve its performance. For fuller details about the mill's history, see D.E.Benney's *Cornish Watermills*.

9 As soon as you have crossed the bridge over the Fal, to complete the 8-mile walk starting at Tregony take the path on the right that runs beside the river. *(Or, for the 5-mile walk starting at Grampound, go straight on through the farm gate, and keep to the obvious track up through the fields - ensuring, please, if you have a dog with you that it is fully under your control. At the minor road described in section 3, turn left for Creed church and Grampound.)* This walk down the wide valley is probably the most attractive part of a route that was already full of delights; and still, as when we were on the farm track that was once a main road, we are reminded of the surprising changes that time brings by this modest watercourse that was once used by cargo vessels. In fact, even some of the tributary streams were navigable if the historian Norden is to be believed. Writing in about 1584, he says, "below Probus church is a rock called *Hayle-boate-rocke,* wherin to this day are many great Iron rynges whereunto Boates have been tyed: Now noe show of a haven, but a little brooke runneth in the valley." "Hayle-boate-rocke", explained by Polsue as "the rock to which boats were hauled", is presumably preserved in the name of Halbote farm, and the little brook that runs through Halbote is the one you crossed just south of Creed (point 3). (It is possible, I suppose, that the "little brooke" is the Fal itself, and Henderson and Coates in *Cornish Bridges and Streams* seem to assume that "Halbot" or "Holbert" rock was in the Fal.) The path runs through woodland for a while and crosses a tiny stream; you have a wooden fence to climb, unless you lower the removable bars (please replace them if you do); and then the path runs beside a hedge on your left, a bit further from the river at this point. At the section where it becomes a grassy track and goes slightly uphill you may encounter some muddy patches. The OS map shows a path through the marshy area near the river, reaching the road beside Tregony Bridge, but we kept to the main one which runs past a row of cottages (Mill Lane) and along Frog Lane to the main street. We nobly resisted the temptation to try one of the Kea House Restaurant's cream teas, but I shan't blame you in the least if you succumb.

Tregony

WALK 4
PORTSCATHO, PENDOWER AND PHILLEIGH
A little over 8 miles. A shorter walk omitting Philleigh is also suggested.

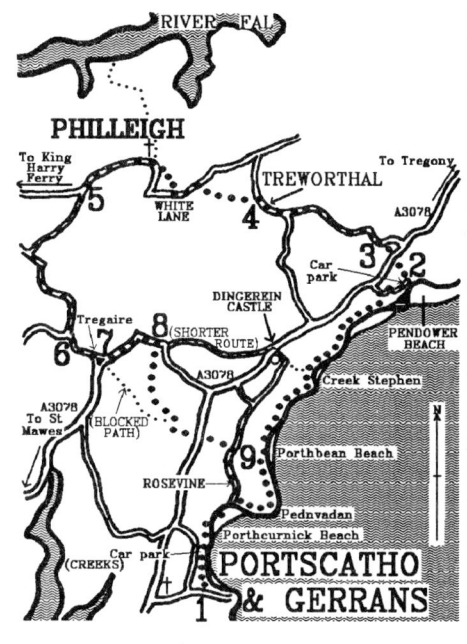

Please don't let "8 miles" frighten you off this one: despite a few ups and downs, mainly along the coast, it's not at all exhausting, and we found it most enjoyable. We took about five hours over it, including a fairly long lunch stop at Philleigh. This is a region of gently rolling hills and long views, both coastal and inland; of picturesque villages and sturdy old farm buildings. A medieval church and an Iron Age fort are on or close to the route. A series of attractive bathing beaches is strung along this section of coast, and refreshments are available at two of them during the season; a pretty and cosy pub well-known locally for good food is very conveniently placed a little over half-way along the route, and when you get back to Portscatho - if you time things well - there's the Plume of Feathers awaiting you. ("Everything that could be asked for in a pub" was David Guthrie's opinion of it.) If that's closed there are shops and seasonal cafés. The shorter route omits Pendower as well as Philleigh and amounts to about four-and-a-half miles. The inland paths are likely to require waterproof footwear (in fact you would be glad of wellies on the path approaching Rosevine: see section 8), and a stick to beat back brambles and other vegetation might prove valuable. The roads included on the route are all minor and usually very quiet ones, with the exception of about a quarter of a mile on the A3078. This is unavoidable at present because of a missing footbridge on a path.

To drive to Portscatho (unless you are using the King Harry Ferry), take the A3078 south from Tregony, turning left where signposted, first at Trewithian and then at Tregassa. Directions are given from the square in Portscatho, but during the season there is little or no long-stay parking down in the village, so use the car park on the left soon after the left turning at Tregassa. This gives you easy access to the coast path less than half a mile north of Portscatho, so if you don't want to visit the village you can shorten the walk slightly by turning left on reaching the cliff edge. There is another car park at Pendower Beach, point 2 in the directions.

PORTSCATHO

Gerrans/Portscatho can obviously be compared with Gorran/Gorran Haven and Levorrick/Porthilly (now combined as Mevagissey): in every case the church was built on high ground some way inland and gathered a village or "churchtown" around it, and a separate community developed at the nearest harbour. The churchtown was usually the older of the pair: Portscatho seems first to have been mentioned in documents in 1592, for example, nearly four centuries later than Gerrans, and Portscatho does not appear on Boazio's map (1597), whereas St Gerans is shown as quite a large village. Laurence O'Toole, however, believes that the two villages "must have grown at about the same pace." *(The Roseland: between River and Sea)* Certainly until this century they preserved very separate identities, even though Portscatho people had to go up to Gerrans for school as well as church. There was a definite boundary line, over which it was foolhardy for Gerrans children to venture after dark. The growth of boat building and especially the boom in pilchard and mackerel fishing meant that the seaside community eventually became the larger of the two, and of course the 20th-century holiday industry has confirmed and quickened that process. The name "Portscatho" means "harbour of boats" (specifically, large rowing-boats), and is locally pronounced "P'scatha" or even just "Scatha". Until 1891 there was no harbour wall, and such protection as there was was provided by ridges of rock near Pencabe Point. During the famous Great Blizzard of that year, however, some of those rocks had to be blasted to enable a wrecked ship, the German steamer *Carl Hirschberg*, to be towed off (with the aid of what a Portscatho lady called "carbolic jacks", according to an excellent but now scarce little book of local people's reminiscences compiled in the 1970s by the Vicar of Gerrans: *The Past in St Gerrans)*, and a short wall was built to replace the rocks. Later it was extended, but still proved a poor substitute, in the opinion of the older local fishermen. Recently Hilary Thomson has published *A History of Gerrans and Portscatho, 1700-1830*. Though academic in approach, it contains a wealth of human detail, painting particularly vivid pictures of the pilchard seining and the smuggling during that period. A map drawn in 1793 shows fish cellars lining almost the whole harbour - probably none too many, however, in view of catches like the one on 14 October 1809, totalling 1700 hogsheads: 51,000 fish. Ms Thomson writes of the evidence of hostility in the village towards the new "Preventive Waterguard" service set up in 1809 to combat smuggling, and tells of men arrested for lighting fires on shore as signals to smugglers. Even when Polsue was compiling his *Lake's Parochial History* (about 1865) the place was apparently still a byword in this respect: "Portscatha," he writes, "is a pretty and pleasantly situated village, and the change from a smuggling cove to a watering-place would be a most congenial one." His wish has, I suppose, come true. For all the bungaloid development, and despite a seafront that strikes Liz Luck as "bland and ugly", it remains "pretty" perhaps partly because it was never "quaint"; and "pleasantly situated" is an understatement. I think Sheila Bird has hit the nail on the head when in *Cornish Villages* she emphasises the special quality of the light here, though I'm less certain what she means by "the dreamy quality of the bay."

WALK 4

1 From Portscatho (*) village square, either walk past the pub (built about 1756 and said to be the village's oldest surviving building) or head towards the slipway, down River Street. Formerly this was called Horse Road, reflecting the fact that it was much used by carts bringing up sand and seaweed for the farms. Take the left turning, where there are coast-path acorn signs. (Toilets are signposted further down River Street.) Soon you are out of the village, and after a few steps up at the National Trust sign "Porthcurnick" you are walking along the edge of the low cliffs, a fine view ahead across Gerrans Bay to Nare Head and Gull Rock with the great bulk of the Dodman in the distance. Near at hand is Porthcurnick Beach, and steps take you down to that. (For the seasonal kiosk and toilets continue ahead up a few steps instead of going down the main flight of steps to the right.) "Porthcurnick" or "Porth Cornick" means "little corner cove". So much sand was removed from this beach by farmers that the sea swept away a group of fishermen's cottages and an old lime kiln. A photograph from the 1890s showing the cottages is in Laurence O'Toole's *The Roseland, Between River and Sea* (1978), which is easily the best book about this area that I know of. From the beach go a few yards up the slipway and turn right through the wooden gate with a NT sign, "Pednavadan". The coast path now heads east for a short distance, providing a good view of Portscatho with the spire of Gerrans church above and Greeb Point in the distance. At Pednvadan *(pental-ban,* literally Brow-peak Head) is a small watch-house, manned in bad weather. Heading north again now, you can see Porthbean ("little cove") Beach with a hotel above, and the coast path takes you down to the beach. We walked here on the last day of 1991, and at that time this beach provided a fine example of the damage plastics can do to our environment; I presume the mess is cleared up each year before many visitors arrive. One of the steeper climbs on this route now follows, and there are a couple more ups and downs before you pass the dome-like green knoll known as the Round House and reach the cove called Creek Stephen. ("Creek" is a form of the Cornish *crug,* a barrow or burial mound. The Round House looks a very likely site for a barrow - and we are close to an undoubted prehistoric site here.)

This is the point at which I suggest you turn inland - following the sign to Curgurrell (another name containing "crug")- if you want to shorten the walk; and if you don't but are interested in seeing the Iron Age earthwork known as Dingerein Castle you might choose to make a short diversion here. The path runs beside Curgurrell Farm and brings you to the road. Continue ahead on that, and just before reaching the main road look over a farm gate on your left for a glimpse of the curved inner rampart of Dingerein Castle (*), close to the main road at the top end of the field. The high hedge beside the road is presumably part of the outer rampart. Return the same way to continue the full walk; otherwise go a few yards right on the main road, then cross and take the road going sharp left, which leads to the Merrose Farm caravan park and so can be quite busy in summer: hence the traffic lights. After a few yards turn left on to the signed bridleway, which runs for about half a mile and makes pleasant walking but can be very muddy towards the far end. At the main road continue ahead (or right) for about 50 yards, and then cross (with great care because of the closeness of a blind bend) to a small stone stile. Now pick up the directions at point 8.

> ### DINGEREIN CASTLE
> Like Resugga (Walk 2) and Carvossa (Walk 3), this is a Celtic Iron Age fort. It had two circular ramparts, but the outer one, which was a little over a hundred yards in diameter, has survived only at the north-western side (adjoining the road corner). The inner one is more complete, but again best-preserved in the north-western part. The ditches have gone completely. Old guide books such as *Murray's Handbook* of 1859 confidently state that an underground passage called the Mermaid's Hole links the earthwork with the shore. A Rector of Ruan Lanihorne at the end of the 18th century decided that the palace of the real or mythical Dark Age King Gerent (said with a hard G) must have been here, so he called the fort Dingerein, "Gerent's castle". The village and bay of Gerrans are also supposed to derive their name from Gerent, although it is possible that the church's patron saint (variously called Gerent, Geren, Gerance, Gerontius, etc.) was another person altogether. For more details about local legends which connect Gerent with prehistoric sites that originated a thousand years or more before his time, see the note on Carne Beacon in Walk 5. Another candidate for the site of Dingerein is the round at Carwarthen, north of St Just; but in fact there is no evidence that there was ever a place called Dingerein in Cornwall.

The coast path continues along the cliff-edge. Beyond the NT sign, "Treluggan Cliffs", you see the Pendower Hotel ahead, and reach it after two more fairly gentle climbs. The coast path turns inland to avoid passing in front of the hotel, where coffee and food are available to non-residents. The road brings you down to the beach car park.

2 Just before reaching the Pendower Beach House Hotel (another source of refreshments during the season), turn left up a rather narrow and steep path where the stick I mentioned in the introductory note may come in handy. Look back for a pretty view of Pendower Beach. After climbing a few steps, walk beside the hedge on your right, crossing a stile near the top of the hill; beyond a second stile, continue in the same line to a third one at the road. Take care when negotiating the quite steep steps down on the far side, because this road tends to carry fast traffic. Cross the road and the stile opposite, following the footpath sign to Treworthal. The path crosses this small field to another stile on the right side of a farm building.

3 Turn left on the minor road, which takes you past several typical Cornish farms, with their mixtures of old and new buildings. Treworlas House is particularly attractive: a nicely restored former farmhouse which we guessed to be late Georgian in date. Names starting with "tre" (=farmstead, estate) usually end with a personal name (normally that of the original owner or farmer). Such is probably the case with Treworlas and the nearby Trevithick; "Treveans", however, means "small farm", and "Treworthal" means "farm on watery ground" or possibly "thicket farm". In fact Treworthal (about half a mile beyond Treveans) is a hamlet rather than a farm, and a very pretty little place, with its thatched cottages, red phone kiosk and Queen Victoria post-box. (We were told that snails have taken up residence in there, so the villagers avoid posting their mail in the evenings!)

Treworthal

4 Just before the last thatched cottage, take the footpath on the left, signed to White Lane and Philleigh. The path, mostly a sunken track with a few stiles, quite soon brings you to another road, opposite a former chapel now converted and extended to form a handsome residence with a fine view including Philleigh Church and a glimpse of the River Fal at Ardevora. The stack of the Trelonk brickworks can be seen. (For details, see Walk 7 in *Around the Fal.*) Turn left. The road runs down through White Lane; just beyond the houses there, take the footpath on the right, signed to Philleigh. It is just to the left of a metal farm gate, and starts at a wooden stile. This path tends to get rather overgrown, and if that proves a problem you could continue to Philleigh on the road instead. The path brings you into the village beside Polglaze ("green pool") Farm, whose small hill of black plastic is perhaps the least charming sight in Philleigh (*). On the left is the early Georgian or Queen Anne Glebe House, formerly the Rectory and now a private residence again after a period as a guest house and restaurant. Continue ahead past the farm, the little school building and the church. *(There is a signed path to the right just before the church, which leads down to a beautiful and peaceful spot beside the River Fal. It makes a worthwhile little diversion, amounting to slightly above a mile there and back, but you are likely to need wellies. The route is clearly indicated with yellow waymark arrows all the way. The earlier part, after you have crossed a couple of stiles, is on farm tracks; then you have to walk diagonally across two*

PHILLEIGH

An old name for the village is Eglosros, "the church in the moorland" or possibly "the Roseland church". The manor, of which nothing now survives, is named "Eglosos" or "Egleshos" in the Domesday Book. The church is dedicated to an unknown saint called Fily; the "Ph" had appeared by 1597, when Baptista Boazio drew his fascinating map of the Fal estuary, and the "eigh" improvement seems to be a later Anglicisation on the model of "Leigh", meaning woodland, clearing or meadow. The castellated church tower is one of the oldest parts of the building, dating from the 13th century. Inside, the font is probably of the same period, and the south arcade ("low and lovely", says Betjeman) was built about two centuries later. Not much else escaped the attentions of the Victorian restorers in 1867: according to Betjeman they "almost rebuilt" the church. The village now seems a very sleepy little place - or rather, it

would be but for the popularity of the Roseland Inn. A century or more ago it presumably had more life of its own, judging by the fact that "A substantial school premises was built adjoining the churchyard in 1860" *(Lake's Parochial History);* and further back than that in time, the road through Philleigh must have been a busy trade route linking West Cornwall with the important port of Tregony via the King Harry Ferry. According to the King Harry Steam Ferry Company's centenary booklet (1988), the road was also part of the Pilgrims' Way to St Michael's Mount. Presumably in medieval or Tudor times travellers were more likely to patronise the inn than are the modern car-drivers trying to catch the quarter-to or the quarter-past.

fields which in 1992 had been ploughed and planted with daffodils, and the path had not been reinstated. Towards the end, where the path dips into woodland, it becomes a sunken lane wide enough for carts to bring coal and other goods from the riverside, where there is a small beach but no sign of a quay. Laurence O'Toole speculates that this may have been "the way the wandering footsteps of St Filius arrived, fourteen hundred years ago.") On the left just before the picture-postcard Roseland Inn, reputed to date from the 16th century, notice what Betjeman describes as "a little Regency Gothick cottage"; it looks rather like two Veryan round houses linked as Siamese twins. Beyond the pub on the right is Court Farm, whose name is perhaps a clue to the site of the old manor house (compare St Stephen and Lanreath, where the manors were called Court, probably in reference to manorial court-leets). Continue along the road for about half a mile. (Walking along this road requires some care, even though it is rarely if ever busy: see the final comment in my note on Philleigh.)

5 Where it bends right, continue ahead along a narrow but tarmacked lane marked "Unsuitable for motors". The truth of this warning emerges after you have passed Trelissa, when it gradually deteriorates to a fairly rough and perhaps muddy track. Gerrans church spire can be seen, and at one point you get a glimpse of the Percuil River. At the T-junction turn left. Soon the track descends - quite steeply at one point - to a ford and footbridge. Lawrence O'Toole describes this "tiny lane" as the only one in Roseland which "has preserved its medieval simplicity." The ford is called Trelissa Watering: horses were tethered to the ring on the bridge while they drank. Finally a short climb brings you to a road.

6 Turn left there. The road climbs past Lanhoose ("grey valley": the house is below, on the right), and at the top of the hill the sea comes back into view. The name of the farm here is Tregaire (*).

TREGAIRE

The name derives from *tre-ker*, "farm of the fort or round". Tregaire Barton stands on a hill and has the sort of wide view usually associated with hill forts, but there is no sign of one here. More surprisingly, there appears to be no relic - not even a carved stone in a farm hedge - of the Chapel of the Holy Cross which was consecrated by Bishop Bronescombe of Exeter in 1463. Tregaire or Tregear was one of the great episcopal manors, given to the Church by King Egbert in the 9th century and listed in Domesday as Tregel. At that time it boasted the unusually large number of sixty teams of oxen (eight to a team). Its lands included the whole of the Roseland peninsula apart from the small manor of Eglosros (see the note on Philleigh), plus St Michael Penkivel parish and parts of Ruan Lanihorne and Feock parishes, and "High Rents" were paid to it from estates as far afield as St Keverne, St Erth and Mevagissey. The map of Tregear Manor drawn by the great Cornish historian Charles Henderson is reproduced in Laurence O'Toole's book. By the end of the 13th century most of the estates had been sold or let as sub-manors. Medieval Bishops of Exeter frequently visited until about 1450; after that, Tregaire became a mere barton, the chapel was eventually desecrated, and now "The farmhouse itself has hardly any ancient features". ("History of the Parish of Gerrans" (1938), included with Canon Doble's account of S.Gerent, recently republished and available in local shops.) Perhaps the only clear sign now of its former importance, apart from a mass of old documents, is the fact that it still has (or had in 1978, according to O'Toole) more land than any other Roseland farm.

---

7 At the main road there should be a footpath straight on, but a combination of barbed wire and a missing footbridge have made it unusable except to the truly intrepid rambler. I have pointed out this problem to the County Footpaths Officer, and in the hope that one day the path will be restored I have shown it with small dots on my map. As things stand, however, you have to turn left and brave the traffic on the A3078. The verge on the far side is helpful, but ironically it disappears where most needed, at the right-hand bends. Continue for about a quarter of a mile, though it will probably seem longer.

8 Don't miss the rather small and somewhat overgrown stone stile on the right, just before a sharp right-hand bend. Cross it and walk along the centre of the field, heading towards the distant spire at Gerrans. The path has a series of stiles, several of which make life difficult by being brambly, awkwardly high, surrounded by mud or all three. After the fourth stile (counting the one at the road as the first) you need to go slightly left to a wooden step-stile and then follow the direction indicated by the yellow arrow, diagonally to the right. At the field corner go through the metal farm gate, walk beside the hedge on your left, and turn left through a second gate just before the farm buildings. This is Pollaughan, "pool of the oxen". The right of way runs beside the farmhouse and along the tarmacked drive to the road. Cross that with care and continue ahead on the path signed "Rosevine". Walk almost straight ahead, but slightly to the right, towards the bungalow. Cross the stile behind a small wooden gate and go down a little to the left to cross a stream. The rather elaborate stile here is made awkward with some wooden bars, and then you are faced with a very muddy patch, churned up by cattle. With the aid of a few stones and bits of wood we managed to cross it more-or-less unscathed, but I can imagine this becoming a real morass during rainy spells. After that little adventure, walk up the slope to join the road via a stile and a fenced path just to the right of the bungalow.

9 Turn right. The road runs gently downhill among the houses and hotels of Rosevine - a pretty name which apparently derives from the Cornish *ros-breyn,* putrid moor. I hasten to add that the name seems to have no relevance nowadays. Laurence O'Toole writes of the remains of a tiny Iron Age settlement found in 1958 at Rosevine by a bungalow owner digging his garden: pottery, a quern for corn-grinding, part of a stone hammer, and remains of shellfish, pigs and sheep. Soon you are back at Porthcurnick Beach, and from there you will know the way back to the car park or down into Portscatho.

Portscatho - from an old photograph

The Fal at Trenowth (Walk 2)

Trewithen House (Walk 3)

Near Portholland (Walk 6)

Chapel Point from Portmellon (Walk 8)

These two photographs were taken within five minutes of each other in October 1991 at Hemmick. Walk 7

Portloe (Walks 5 and 6)

The valley path between Mevagissey and Heligan (Walk 9)

WALK 5
VERYAN, PORTLOE AND NARE HEAD
About nine miles - but several shorter versions are suggested, ranging from about four-and-a-half to seven-and-a-half miles.

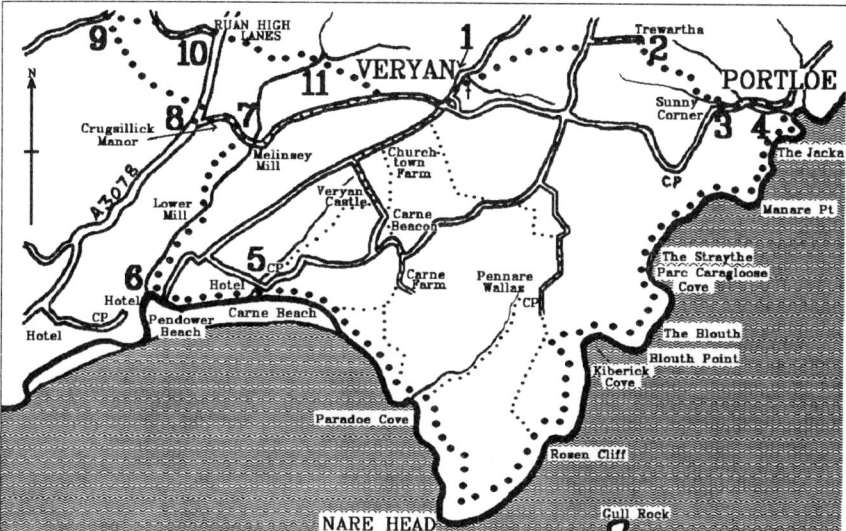

This walk is based on one of Cornwall's loveliest inland villages and also includes one of the most unspoilt fishing havens. The inland walking is pleasant and mostly away from roads; the coastal section is spectacular and in places quite strenuous. You will need to be prepared for mud, and there are one or two places on the cliffs which require particular care. The path running through the valley above Pendower Beach is sometimes rather overgrown. Veryan and Portloe both have public toilets, pubs and shops, and the shop at Portloe also serves coffee, teas and other refreshments during the season; there is a general store at the filling station at Ruan High Lanes. There are several good beaches along the way, but some of them are accessible only by scrambling. If you are planning to take a dog, be sure to keep it on a lead, especially along the coast path, where farmers' notices warn of the drastic measures taken against dogs that worry sheep. A bewilderingly large number of attractive circular routes around Nare Head could be devised, especially now that the National Trust has opened up new paths, or made old ones available to the public, and there are car parks at Portloe, close to Nare Head near Pennare Wallas Farm, and at Carne and Pendower beaches, so that you can quite easily plan your walk to enable you to have a pub lunch at Veryan or Portloe, for example. A combination of the National Trust's "Coast of Cornwall" Leaflet No. 20 and the OS "Pathfinder" map should enable you to work out even more routes if you need them!

Veryan (*) is signposted from the A3078 south of Tregony. There is usually plenty of space for parking near the school and public toilets, opposite the main entrance to the church.

VERYAN

"A Cornish delight in a leafy dell", it was called by Arthur Mee, and Betjeman describes it as a "mild tropic garden". It is best known for its five round houses, four of them thatched, built early in the 19th century by a wealthy and vigorous Vicar, Jeremiah Trist. (Not that he needed to be particularly wealthy to do so: apparently one pair of round houses cost under £70 to build.) The cross on the top of each perhaps helped to encourage the local tradition that the purpose of the circular shape was to deny the devil any corner to hide in, or to fool him into being unable to find the entrance to the village. Christine North, in her excellent history of Veryan, is sceptical about this and other legends about them, remarking simply that "The Houses were built to a "rustic" design fashionable at the time and enhanced the appearance of Trist's extensive property in the village." The most impressive example of that was (and is) Parc Behan, the house near Veryan Green, north of the churchtown, which he built for himself about 1810. It now belongs to the National Trust and has been divided into flats. Many of the trees in the "leafy dell" date from the time when the Trists were landscaping the village. For a detailed account of the three generations of the Trist family who dominated life in Veryan from 1773 to 1869, see Christine North's article in the 1980 *Journal of the RIC*. The principal Domesday manor of Veryan was Elerky or Elerkey, whose owners have included the Lercedekne family, associated with the building of the castle at Ruan Lanihorne (see *Around the Fal*, Walk 6), and the Tregians of Golden (see Walk 3 in this book). The manor house has long gone, but the McLeod Water Garden may perhaps mark the site of its swannery: the name Elerky means swan or swanpool. The church includes Norman features, with 13th- and 15th-century additions; it was restored in the 1840s and again in 1897-8, but less harshly than many other Cornish churches. A wall monument worth looking for is that of Admiral Kempe, who sailed with Captain Cook and was at Quebec with Wolfe. A descendant of his, who made or inherited a fortune from a cough mixture called "Liquafruta", bequeathed money to build and maintain a group of houses in Veryan for the widows of Cornish seamen. The dedication of the church to St Symphorian probably explains the name of the village: by the 16th century the name was being written as "Severian", and that eventually turned into "St Veryan". Symphorian was a Burgundian, martyred in the 3rd century; various theories have been put forward as to how his name came to be linked with this place. Some say that the saint behind the name is actually Berriona, a 6th-century Irish virgin who is supposed to have cured the son of King Geraint when he was paralysed. (See the notes on Carne Beacon in this walk and Dingerein Castle in Walk 4.) Veryan's Holy Well, now dry, stands opposite the church; it was restored in 1912.

1 The walk begins just to the left of the war memorial as you look towards the church. There is a Public Footpath sign (Portloe via Trewartha), but it may be hidden by leaves. The path passes through the small memorial gardens with their pond; after a kissing gate you pass through a children's play area. Cross the bridge at the far right-hand corner of this. After the

WALK 5

Veryan

stile, make for another stile you will see beside a small wood to your right, but do not cross it. Instead, walk on up the field, heading for the top-left corner, where you will find a small iron gate. (The large house to your left, by the way, is Parc Behan, mentioned in the note on Veryan.) Go through the gate, over the stile on the other side of the patch of woodland, and continue straight on across the field, aiming for the farm buildings. After the 7-bar gate, the lane brings you past a former Methodist chapel to a road. Here turn left and then immediately right, still following the public footpath to Portloe. The headland now coming into view on the horizon is the Dodman.

2 At the farm entrance (Trewartha Hall) turn left through the metal gate, and when you come to two more gates go through the one on the left. Keep by the hedge on your right till you reach the kissing gate - a tight squeeze if you've got a back-pack, and perhaps even if not! Now head for the buildings in the valley bottom and go through the gate on the left by the first cottage. You then pass in front of the cottage and through a communal garden area. This is "Sunny Corner", even in the rain. Up to the right are the remains of a watermill, and the sluice gate just to your left as you approach the road shows that this is a tailings leat rather than a natural stream. A millstone decorates the entrance to Spear-Point opposite.

3 Cross the bridge on the road and turn left, down past the Ship Inn into Portloe (*). The long, low old building on the right just below the Ship was, the pub's landlord told me, used as a coal store within living memory, but may possibly have been a pilchard cellar before that. At the bottom fork right for the Lugger Hotel (which also offers bar food, but only during the season), the public toilets and the small harbour.

WALK 5

PORTLOE

The name probably means "harbour of an inlet". Despite its popularity as a place to visit, Portloe has kept much of its character as a fishing village, mainly, I suppose, because there's so little room for "development" in what Liz Luck calls its "cramped and dramatic" situation, huddled around its tiny harbour at the bottom of steep hills. The original lifeboat house of 1869 was replaced by All Saints Church; the later one, more conveniently situated down by the water, became an infants' school four years after the lifeboat station was closed in 1887, and later the village institute. The fish cellars have gone - some of them stood on what is now The Lugger's car park -, but two limekilns are near the church (the left-hand one is particularly well preserved, but unfortunately seems to double as the village litter-bin), and there are remains of others up by The Ship. Which of these kilns was the scene of an accident reported in *The West Briton* in July 1841, I don't know: "On Sunday, the 4th instant, a little girl, about five years old, daughter of Mr Paine, of the Coast Guard, at Portloe, was unfortunately burnt to death, by attempting to take a roasted potatoe from a lime-kiln." In 1855 the village had two inns: The Ship, locally nicknamed "The Drinking Kitchen", rebuilt in 1904 after a fire; and the New Inn, which, I believe, became The Lugger. Portloe shares with most of the other south coast villages a long history of smuggling, dating back at least to the 17th century when the famous smuggler and pirate Robert or Robin Long lived at Veryan, and still thriving in 1843 (I mean the smuggling, not Robin Long, who is said to have ended his days hanging in chains at Bessybeneath, where the road to Veryan leaves the A3078) when the coastguards recovered over forty barrels of liquor which had been anchored to the sea bed: the anchor-ropes got caught up in a fisherman's hooks.

4 The coast path heading south and west leaves Portloe a few yards below the toilets. *(An alternative way up to the cliffs, avoiding The Jacka and a rather uncomfortably steep little downward slope, is the path that starts beside the toilets.)* You now climb The Jacka, which provides you with fine views over the village, but it's especially here that you need to tread carefully: the path goes perilously close to the edge just past the seat. After a steep little drop, followed by quite a steep climb, bear left where the path forks, keeping to the cliff edge. At Manare Point, where there are two stiles in quick succession, you will see Parc Camels and Parc Caragloose Coves below you. "Parc" means "field". "Camels", the name of a hamlet nearby, means "curved shore" or "crooked cliff", and "Caragloose" appears in various forms along the Cornish coast: Carrick Lûz (Lizard) and Cataclews (near Padstow), for example. It means "grey rock". The island ahead has a name even more frequently found: Gull Rock. It achieved fame and glory during the 1950s as a set in a film of *Treasure Island* (the same film included other scenes shot at Pill Creek, Feock); before that Gull Rock was perhaps best known for the wreck of the German ship *Hera* in 1914. The nineteen who died are buried in Veryan churchyard. After you pass Broom Parc House and its small pines the path winds down, and at the lowest point you are only a few feet above the rocks. These are called The Straythe, referring to the stream you have just crossed (Cornish, *streyth,* stream). The Straythe was the scene of a shipwreck during the great blizzard of 1891. The *Dundella* was carrying a cargo of fruit, and if you are given a painful bite as you pass it may be that you have been attacked by what locals used to call "a Dundella fly". People believed the flies hatched from rotten pineapples left on board, and plagued the area ever since. Bites or no bites, it's a hard slog now up to the cliffs known as The Blouth (probably from the Cornish *blogh,* bald, bare). A couple of small beaches you see below as you climb, which look accessible only by boat, were, when we were last here, a good illustration of the harm that can be done to our landscape by multicoloured plastics. At the southern end of The Blouth is Blouth Point, overlooking Kiberick Cove, with a beach that looks almost equally inaccessible from the cliffs. "Kiberick" may derive from the Cornish word for timber - perhaps a hint of a long-forgotten shipwreck.

For the shortest way back to Veryan, take one of the paths inland to the National Trust's car park near Pennare Wallas (Lower Pennare farm), which is visible from the coast path as you approach from above Kiberick. The first is the shortest of all: simply take the path on the right after following the coast path round to the head of the valley above Kiberick Cove. Secondly, you could continue to Rosen ("little promontory") Cliff and take the track north from there, with a cattle grid at the start. You can recognise this place by the very sheer cliff on your left, with Gull Rock at about its closest. Beside the coast path are a disused World War II bunker and (to quote the NT leaflet) "the ventilators of an underground Royal Observer Corps station". I wonder what they observe down there. A third possibility - and the best - is to go on around Nare Head to Paradoe Cove and walk up the delightful wooded valley to the car park from there. Beyond the car park you continue north for about half a mile on a surfaced road, and then take the footpath signposted to Veryan, on the left where the road bends sharply right. After crossing the stile, go by the hedge on the left, over a fence-like stile, then across to the hedge opposite. Walk with that on your left; when you come to a gap with a low wooden fence cross to the next field and go on with the hedge on your right. Cross a track, go through a small gate and continue beside the hedge to the corner, where stiles help you up and over a high hedge. Turn left on the road. After the farm entrance, cross the stile on the right. The path crosses the field, cutting off the right-hand corner. Cross the double stile and walk down the long field, roughly in the centre, to a further stile; then go straight on, with a wire fence on your right. At the road turn right for the centre of Veryan.

From Nare Head (*) you have fine views of the Dodman in the east (and as

---

NARE HEAD

Like Nare Point on the other side of the Helford, its name merely means "headland", being a shortened form of Penare or Pennare, the names of nearby farms. There is another Penare Farm at Dodman Point, suggesting that that too was once called Nare. The Nare Head on this walk has belonged to the National Trust since 1931; until then it was the property of the Williams family of Caerhays.

far as Rame Head, near Plymouth, in really clear conditions) to the Manacles and Lowland Point in the west, with Portscatho across Gerrans Bay in the middle distance. Another quite strenuous section of the coast path follows, particularly at Paradoe Cove (pronounced "Perarda"), a beautiful spot, complete with stream and a lonely building which estate agents would describe as an ideal opportunity for the handyman. The NT leaflet tells the story of the fisherman called Mallet who built it early in the 19th century. A cave nearby is called Tregagle's Hole, one of many Cornish places associated with the doomed, wandering spirit who howls or moans in anguish among the rocks and on the bleak moors - a spirit represented in the mythologies of many lands, but in Cornwall given the name of an actual person, a wicked steward from Trevorder, near St Breock. (His family was called Tregeagle, but the spelling "Tregagle" shows how the name is said.) (See *Around Padstow*, Walk 5.) Just beyond Paradoe Cove is a spot I remember from a walk here back in May 1988, when there was a breathtaking display of multicoloured flowers, with bluebells, campion, foxgloves, the dark red spikes of docks, the tall yellow heads of wild cabbage, the whites of stitchwort and cow parsley, plus the inevitable dandelions and buttercups, all shining out through the tall, feathery grasses and the bright new fronds of bracken. Where the path divides, keep left for the cliff path to Carne Beach, *but fork right, following the yellow arrow on the acorn post, to return to Veryan via Carne Beacon, thus completing a round walk of just over six miles. At the T-junction turn right. After passing among the buildings of Carne Farm, continue ahead at the road, and where*

The ruins of Mallet's cottage at Paradoe Cove

> ### CARNE BEACON
> This is one of the most impressive prehistoric remains in Cornwall, a Bronze Age round barrow of unusually large proportions in a very commanding position on a hill 370 feet above sea level. ("Carne" itself means barrow, and it has been used as one of the chain of beacons along the south coast.) Not surprisingly, there is an ancient tradition that it was the burial place of a king, specifically the 6th- or 8th-century King Gerent, Gerennius or Geraint, after whom Gerrans and Dingerein Castle (at Curgurrel, north of Portscatho: Walk 4) are said to be named. Excavation revealed a stone burial chest but none of the rich grave goods that might be expected of a royal interment, let alone the golden ship with silver oars that the legend claims was buried with him. The barrow, of course, predates Gerent by something between 1600 and 3000 years.

the road bends left still go on in the same direction, crossing the stile signposted Churchtown Farm. The path goes along the left side of the burial mound on top of Carne Beacon (*) and then straight on, crossing two stiles. The official path cuts across the field, reaching the road via a stile just to the left of the farm buildings. Turn right at the road, and you soon enter Veryan between two of its famous round houses.

5 The coast path emerges on to a road just above Carne Beach. There are toilets in the National Trust car park.

Yet another possible and worthwhile route back to Veryan is via Veryan Castle (*). For this, take the permissive path which starts at the inland end of the NT car park. After crossing the stile to the right of the gate, follow the line indicated by the signpost: up to the hedge on the right and over the stile to the right of the 5-bar gate. Now the flat platform of the earthwork is to your left, commanding a fine view of the valley and the bay, with a glimpse of the Goonhilly Downs dishes on the skyline. Beyond the earthwork the path crosses a stone stile and runs beside the hedge on your right. From here there is a good view left to "china-clay country", and close at hand to the right is the barrow that marks the top of Carne Beacon. Turn left on the road and right at the T-junction for Veryan.

For the longer walks, continue along the coast to Pendower Beach: the quickest way is along the foreshore, if the tide allows. Above the beaches is the Nare Hotel, and above that Gwendra ("white sands") Farm, now holiday accommodation. Gwendra is one of the few places in Cornwall where limestone has been quarried in useful quantities. Presumably it was burnt in

> ### VERYAN CASTLE
> This earthwork, probably the remains of an Iron Age settlement, has a very unusual setting: instead of the usual hilltop or promontory site, it was built on a slope which had to be excavated in order to provide a level platform, with a steep drop on the west side. The remains of a bank and ditch can be seen on the uphill side. The site has not been the subject of an archaeological "dig", so nothing is known about the dwellings which presumably existed, not only within the main enclosure but possibly also outside it, since there are traces of outer defences on the east side. Local names for the site are Veryan Rings and the Ringarounds.

the two kilns at Pendower whose ruins have survived. As I write this (September 1991) there has been a reminder of the long tradition of smuggling in these parts by the discovery of packets of cannabis resin on Pendower Beach. "Pendower" means "foot of the water", referring presumably to the stream beside which the next part of the walk runs.

6 Don't go as far as the Pendower Beach Hotel, but from the beach car park take the bridleway up the valley, just to the right of the stream. At Lower Mill (Melinsey Cottages) go through the courtyard and over the footbridge. The path continues quite steeply up through the woodland. This part of the walk tends to be overgrown, with a fair proportion of nettles, and a stout pair of trousers would be an advantage. The path reaches a road at Melinsey Mill, whose name means "mill-house". This and the Lower Mill were the manor mills of Elerky: see the note about Veryan. The ruins of Melinsey Mill ("surely one of the smallest mills in Cornwall", according to D.E.Benney's *Cornish Watermills*) are a few yards along the road to the right; its waterwheel - made at Harris and Polmear's City Foundry, Truro, in 1882 - is still in place, though sadly decayed.

7 One last choice of route presents itself here: either turn right and return to Veryan on this narrow and in places steep road (it carries a moderate amount of traffic, so you need to take care); or for a route that is mainly on paths, passing through pleasant but not outstandingly attractive countryside, turn left. This soon brings you past Crugsillick Manor, whose name means "Sillick's barrow": the OS map indicates a tumulus close by, on the right side of the road.

8 At the main road turn right, then take the footpath on the left, signposted to Treworgan, which starts at a gate less than a hundred yards on. Follow the line of the hedge straight on, and go through the second gate or gap on the right. Now head for the farm - not the closest group of buildings, to the left, but the older-looking ones with a lane leading towards them. Go down to the field corner by the lane. To get on to the lane you may need to step over a low wire fence at the field entrance. The lane takes you past the farm and brings you to a crossroads.

9 Now take the footpath on the right; it cuts diagonally across the field to a stile near the far right-hand corner. Turn right at the road, which brings you to Ruan High Lanes, where there is a garage with a shop where you can buy provisions.

10 At the T-junction turn left, signposted Truro, and then immediately right on to the footpath to Veryan, which starts as a narrow path up some steps and over a decaying wooden stile. Keep the hedge on your left at first, but after the second stone stile cross the stile on your left and continue with the hedge on your right. The path goes down into the valley, keeping left of the woodland.

11 After crossing the stream by a slate bridge, climb the steps and go straight up over the ridge of the field to where you will see a wrought-iron gate. Go through that and make for the three trees at the field corner. Here a stile returns you to the road. Turn left for Veryan. By now the New Inn will probably be a welcome sight!

WALK 6
PORTHOLLAND AND PORTLOE,
with a possible extension to
CAERHAYS CHURCH AND CASTLE
*About four and a half miles,
or a little over seven miles with the extension.
Could be done as two separate walks.*

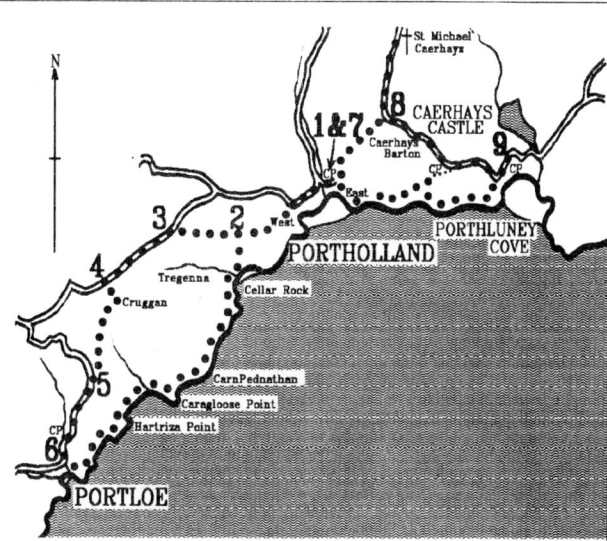

If Portloe has escaped the worst consequences of being a magnet to holidaymakers, Portholland, despite its attractive setting and good beach, miraculously seems to be completely unspoilt by tourism - though it does at least acknowledge its existence by providing toilets and a car park. There is also a tiny shop. The inland route that starts this walk takes you through typical Cornish coastal farming country, and the going here is easy, apart from the initial long climb. Nearly a mile is on roads, normally very quiet, although there may be quite a lot of traffic on the road up from Portloe during the season. The path south of Cruggan had been ploughed and not reinstated when I last walked it, so good, watertight footwear is advisable. At Portloe you will find more toilets, another shop, this time doubling as a café, and two pubs, though one of those (The Lugger) is likely to be closed out of season. The Ship is a little way up the hill on the far side of the village. The walk back to Portholland along the coast is a fine one, but be prepared for several long, steep climbs. A couple of short stretches are, in fact, unusually steep, and might be quite hard to manage if you were walking in the opposite direction and had to descend them. The walk from Portholland to Caerhays is interesting and makes a good contrast. It starts with a long inland climb, but the return coastal walk is comparatively easy. You could shorten this walk in several ways: by omitting the church, or the castle at Porthluney Cove, or even both! An attractive possibility would be to start, reasonably early in the morning, with the Caerhays walk (point 7) and continue to Portloe in time for lunch plus a rest to recharge your batteries for the rigours (and splendours) of the coast.

WALK 6

The directions start at the car park in East Portholland. To drive there from St Austell, take the A390 west towards Truro and fork left just beyond Hewas Water towards Tregony (B3287). The winding and narrow road that eventually reaches the coast at East Portholland is the second left turning from that. From Truro, leave the A390 just beyond Tresillian, taking the A3078 Tregony/St Mawes road. About 2 miles beyond Tregony follow the sign (left) for Veryan; then it's first left, first right and first left again. This road brings you to the coast at West Portholland, where there is a small parking space overlooking the beach, but for the main car park, toilets and shop turn sharp right, down into East Portholland.

1 From the main car park in Portholland (*), you could cross the beach to the coast path westwards at low tide; it is not advisable to try scrambling along the rocks and concrete sea defences below the cliffs: a notice at the other end warns that the cliffs are very unstable. Otherwise walk back up the road past the toilets, turning sharp left to West Portholland and left again at the Methodist Chapel. Notice the well-preserved pair of limekilns, behind the lifebuoy and an old winch. Cross the stream and climb the steps on the right. This part of the coast path heads a little way inland, climbing quite steeply for several hundred yards with a valley down to your right.

2 When you come to a signpost, leave the coast path by continuing straight ahead on the Public Byway to Morvah. Here the path is being invaded by Japanese knotweed, a very rampant plant which seems to thrive on most herbicides. At the bungalows, bear left along the tarmacked lane.

3 At the road, go left and continue for about half a mile, ignoring the left turning to Tregenna. (The sign advertising Veryan Vineyard might well, however, tempt you to go and investigate. Opening times were, in 1991, given as from 2 to 6 every day except Sunday. From Tregenna there is a footpath to Cruggan, so you would not need to return to the road.)

PORTHOLLAND

Portholland consists of little more than a chapel, a smallholding and a few fishermen's cottages around two small coves, each with its stream. The smallholding, complete with pond, ducks, geese, hens and doves, still seems to be thriving, but there's little if any fishing now: despite the lack of obvious commercialisation (a result, I presume, of the influence of the Williams family of Caerhays), the hamlet is probably just as dependent on the holiday business as others along the Cornish coast. In the early 1960s John Betjeman formed the impression that the cottages are "summer hide-outs"; if it was true then it's hardly likely to be less so thirty years later. East Portholland's Methodist chapel, now 110 years old, is sadly neglected-looking and not as yet "converted", but the one overlooking the other cove is still in use. The name is pronounced *Portholland* (rather than *Porth-olland)*. An old version of it is Portallan; the meaning is uncertain, but possibly the main stream was once known as the Allan or Allen, which is certainly found elsewhere in Cornwall as a river name. The River Allen, for example, flows through Truro, and Alan is the old name for the River Camel.

WALK 6

Limekilns at Portholland

4 Turn left to Cruggan farm, one of the many place names in Veryan parish which derives from the Cornish *cruc,* barrow or hillock. In many cases, though not all, this indicates a prehistoric burial mound; none is marked on the "Pathfinder" map here, but such features have often been ploughed out, and this is the more likely at Cruggan because the name probably comes from *criggan,* the diminutive form of the word. Follow the concrete drive round to the right, through the gate into the farmyard. Bear left, passing between the farmhouse and the other main building; here another farm gate, with an old footpath sign beside it, brings you to a lane. Soon you cross a wall by steps into a field where the path may have been ploughed up. A sign directs you to head for the bungalow, that is, the nearest building; this means crossing the field, heading slightly to your right. At the left side of the bungalow there is a kissing gate which brings you to a road.

5 Turn left and continue down the road into Portloe. There is a note about the village in Walk 5. Unless you have done that walk already or plan to, it would be worth climbing to the top of "The Jacka", the cliff above the harbour on the far side, for the fine view of the village.

6 The coast path back to Portholland is clearly signposted. It takes you past the Methodist Chapel and a beautifully restored mill. The waterwheel has gone, but the leat, complete with sluice gate, is still there, and you can see where a channel has been cut for it in the rocks below. The path runs in front of a row of cottages, then up steps, past "The Flagstaff", and behind the coastguard lookout hut. One might guess that the fishermen's "huer's hut" was at The Flagstaff; it also looks like the ideal site for the Watch House that was built for the preventive officers at Portloe: see Mary Waugh's *Smuggling in Devon & Cornwall 1700-1850*. The National Trust's leaflet, however, refers to "an early type of coastguard lookout". As you descend from there, the view ahead embraces Caragloose Point, Porthluney Cove, Hemmick Beach and the Dodman. Above Hartriza Point a pile of smallish rocks and rubble lies beside and across the path: was this someone's deliberate attempt to block it? After a steepish climb with steps, the path descends to Caragloose Point, where the "grey rocks" almost form an island, and a complete island, Shag Rock, is just offshore. From here you can see Manacle Point, fifteen or more miles south west on the Lizard peninsula. The long and in places steep climb that follows takes you to Carn Pednathan, probably meaning "birds'-tor head". Now it's down again, through an attractive little wooded patch, to the valley and cove below Tregenna, with its two footbridges. The beach is still a little way below and not easy to reach, but the OS map names "Cellar Rock" down there, which suggests that it was a place for landing fish or contraband or both. Once more the path climbs, this time heading inland, thus missing Perbargus ("buzzard cove"?) Beach and Point. Soon you are back among the Japanese knotweed and on the path by which you originally left Portholland. If you use the road to get back to East Portholland, notice how the limekilns were sited in such a way that the limestone could easily be loaded from above.

7 From the car park at East Portholland walk up past the row of cottages on the seaward side of the post office, each protected from stormy seas with double doors, and follow the acorn sign to the left, beside the sea wall. At the next sign, continue straight on, signposted to St Michael Caerhays, up the side of the valley. As you go, you will have plenty of time to admire the views of village and coast, and to reflect how much longer one-third of a mile is than it sounds! Don't be surprised if pheasants rise with a squawk and a clatter of wings from the hedges and fields: you are skirting the Caerhays estate. Cross the stile on your right, then walk with the hedge on your left until passing through the gap in it. Go through the five-bar gate, and then head for the telegraph pole; when a bungalow comes into view aim just to the right of it. Here there are two stiles, the first made rather awkward to cross by barbed wire, even though the barbs were wrapped in blue plastic.

8 At the road, turn right for Caerhays Castle and Porthluney Cove; but to visit St Michael Caerhays Church (*) turn left. On the way you will pass the gatehouse to the castle, and later a commemorative oak tree, dating (like

> ### ST MICHAEL CAERHAYS CHURCH
>
>
>
> It is worth walking round to the north side of the church, not only for the view of the Caerhays estate, but also to see the very old doorway, now blocked up, with a carving of the Lamb above it. The church guide refers to this as "Pre-Norman". Inside, very little of the ancient workmanship survived what Betjeman calls the "vile" restoration (1864), but there are still some old stained glass and memorial tablets to the Trevanion family of Caerhays, plus a life-size statue of Captain George Byron Bettesworth (1785-1808), who was a member of that family. The Trevanions were, as the Captain's name implies, related to the poet, Lord Byron.

me) from 1937 but still no great size (unlike me). Having recently read Anne Treneer's description of the gardens of Caerhays village in *School House in the Wind,* I was surprised at the rather bleak place we found. The disused school, set back behind ugly walls, was "To Let" when we last walked here. Presumably all the buildings still belong to the Squire, and I suppose their rather drab and stark uniformity reflects the taste of his forebears. (Could they really have admired those brick porches?) The unpretentious little church is all the more charming by contrast, and the members of the tiny congregation who were emerging from mattins gave us a friendly welcome. They assured us that the rusty bracket over the church door was not actually a relic of a netball court but once supported an oil lamp. Return the same way. The large farm on your right as you start the descent to the cove is Caerhays Barton, another unappealing group of buildings, dominated by concrete and "galvanise". If you do not want to go right down to the beach and castle (and they are both on the route of Walk 7), you could go through the wooden gate at the far end of the parking-space on the right; if you go right from there on the upper path, you soon join the coastal footpath, avoiding a steepish climb in the process. For information about Caerhays, see Walk 7.

9 From Porthluney Cove, return up the road, and where it bends right go up the steps ahead, signposted to East Portholland. The coast path runs by the cliff edge at first, passing quite close to Watchouse Point, overlooking Porthluney - presumably another indication of the efforts made by the preventives to cope with smuggling. Before long, at a field corner the coast path turns a little way inland: you have to walk up to a gate, and this is the link with the path starting at the small car park, as mentioned earlier. From here on, all is straightforward and easy walking.

WALK 7
CAERHAYS, GORRAN AND DODMAN POINT
Nearly eight miles.
Several shorter versions are possible.

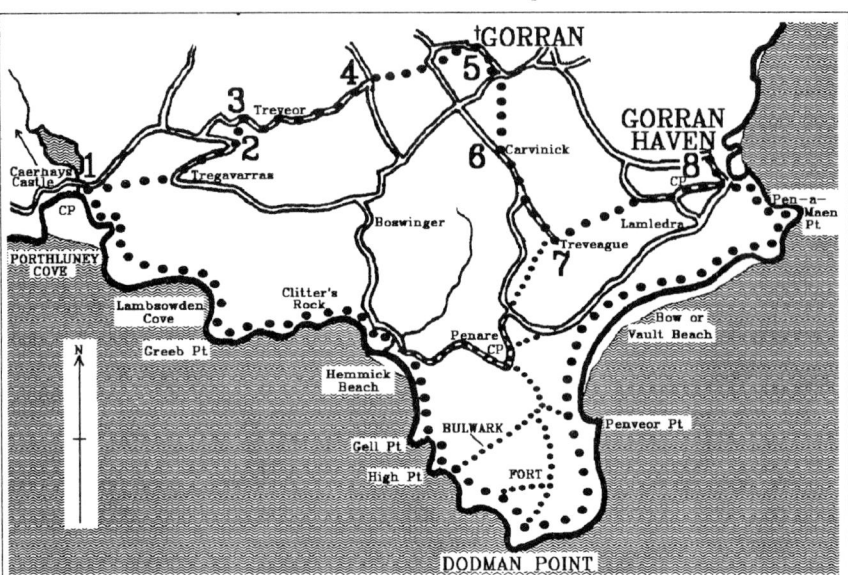

This is definitely a walk to occupy a full day unless you are experienced in coping with the ups-and-downs of the coast path - although in fact the coastal walking between Gorran Haven and Dodman Point is fairly level. The full walk offers a splendid variety of inland and coastal scenery, along with a unique country house set in beautifully landscaped grounds, plus two attractive old villages, perhaps the most impressive prehistoric rampart in Cornwall, and several good bathing beaches. Like Nare Head (Walk 5), Dodman Point offers a great number of attractive "round walks", some of which could include Gorran Churchtown, Gorran Haven or Caerhays, and if you prefer one of these instead of the full route, I suggest you use the Penare car park. There are pubs and shops at Gorran Churchtown and Gorran Haven.

Directions are given from Porthluney Cove (Caerhays Castle), which might be the best point to start the full walk, because it would enable you to get refreshments almost half-way along the route at Gorran Haven. For a medium-length walk omitting Caerhays you could park at Gorran Haven, reading the directions from point 8, and return via Penare and Treveague (see points 6 and 7); and for a walk round the Dodman alone use the National Trust car park at the beautiful old farm of Penare (grid reference SW 999404). Footpaths to Vault Beach and to Dodman Point are signposted from Penare. All these places are best approached by car from the road south from St Austell to Gorran Haven: consult your map!

WALK 7

1 Close to the gatehouse to Caerhays Castle (*) (the note and sketch are overleaf), cross the little bridge, go through the kissing gate and follow the sign pointing to Tregavarras. Walk just to the right of the clump of trees, mainly holm oaks. From here you get a fine view back over the lake and Porthluney Cove, named from the River Luney, which rises near Ventonwyn Mine, west of Sticker. "Luney" probably means "smooth, even". The path continues up over the field to a stile on the right of a farm gate near the top-right corner. (If the field contains beautiful but fearsome-looking Highland cattle with long horns, don't panic: they seem to be always very placid.) Turn left on the road.

2 Where the road bends left, go straight on, marked Footpath to Treveor, past a row of cottages. After the stile, keep by the hedge on the left at first, then cross stepping stones over a boggy patch to another stile and a footbridge. (Watch your steps here: the planks are getting old, and plant growth may hide the gaps between them.) Now go up over the ridge to a stile at the top corner, where there's another fine view.

3 Turn right on the road and continue past Treveor, with its lakes on the right. "Treveor" means "big farm", a name that suits it better than "Penveor" suits the rather small headland north of the Dodman; but Treveor is now less of a farm and more of a campsite.

4 At the T-junction turn left then immediately right over a stile, signed to Gorran. Head slightly left of the church to a stile, cross the road to the next stile, then a third and fourth; at the road in Gorran Churchtown turn right, past (or to!) the pub. See Walk 8 for a note about the church and village.

5 When you are ready to continue, go on along the main road, and after a few yards use the new footpath up on the right, presumably intended mainly for use by the village schoolchildren. At the road continue straight on through Menagwins ("windy hill") Farm, following the sign to Carvinick. Cross the stile on the left of the farm gate. Now the path goes diagonally to the right, across the field. Look right to see the modern school buildings which replaced those described by Anne Treneer, burnt down in 1967. After two more stiles head towards the farm buildings of Carvinick ("stony camp" - compare The Winnick at Pentewan). Here it's best to go through the first gate into the farmyard, because the mud around the second one can be spectacular. Go to the road on the right.

6 Turn left on the road, and where it bends right go straight on towards Treveague Farm, whose outbuildings have been converted to holiday accommodation. (This farm was advertised for sale in *The West Briton* in 1814, described as "very advantageous for manure, being a quarter of a mile from Gorran-Haven, where lime, sand, ore-weed, caff-fish, and old salt, may be had in the greatest abundance." Caff-fish were pilchards unfit for sale, and the "old salt" had been used for curing fish.) *To return to Caerhays without walking to Gorran Haven and possibly cutting out the Dodman too, take the signed path to Penare, through a gate on the right just before Treveague. The path goes across the field through another gate with a footpath sign, then straight on via two more gates to a road. Still continue*

WALK 7

Porthluney Cove and Caerhays Castle as seen at the start of this walk

CAERHAYS CASTLE

It was designed by John Nash, the architect of Buckingham Palace, and replaced a 16th-century mansion which was demolished in 1808. The cost of building it and landscaping the grounds helped to bring ruin on the Trevanion family; their love of gambling also contributed. To quote from Christine Hawkridge's *A History of Gorran*, "The last Trevanion left the ancestral home stealthily by the back door while the bailiffs were approaching the front. The castle remained empty for many years and was robbed of all its movable furnishings. The papier-mâché roofs recommended by Mr Nash were not adequate to cope with Cornish rain, and the roof collapsed, the rain came in, and a family of ducks were observed to be swimming happily in a large puddle on the drawing-room floor." The Williams family (the mining millionaires of Scorrier House: see *The Landfall Book of the Poldice Valley* and other books of mine), who have owned it since 1852, have restored its original Gothick splendour, and thanks largely to the plant-hunting expeditions sponsored by John Charles Williams (1861-1939) its garden is now known throughout Britain, if not further afield, especially for its rhododendrons and other oriental plants. The grounds cover about sixty acres. Usually the gardens are opened to the public two or three times a year: see the current *Gardens of Cornwall Open Guide*.

straight on. From Penare you could join the coast path above Vault Beach, at Penveor Point, at the Dodman, near High Point or at Hemmick Beach: see the map. For Hemmick continue down the road past the NT car park.

7 For the full walk, turn left past Treveague House and go through the metal farm gate (footpath sign: Gorran Haven). The path takes you down an attractive valley. Cross the stream by the stepping stones, go down through the gate, bear left on the gravelled drive, and at the road turn right to go down into Gorran Haven. See the note about this in Walk 8. (If you want the pub - the Llawnroc Inn - go down to the beach, turn left up Church Street and left again up Chute Lane.)

8 From the pub, return to the harbour and turn left at Foxhole Lane. The coast path starts up some steps, signposted to Vault Beach. From here on, few directions are needed; I'll just mention some points of interest, a few possible complications in the route, and some alternative routes that would shorten the walk. As you approach the first headland (Pen-a-maen, "stone head"), either continue around the edge or take the high path. The latter involves some scrambling, both up and down, but rewards you with a good view, and there is also an interesting memorial tablet set in the rock. The large house you soon see up on the right is Lamledra; a road runs from this parallel with the coast path, and this road is closest when you get near to the end of the long beach (called Bow Beach for an obvious reason, or Vault Beach for no reason I know, though it is popularly supposed to be a gloomy link with the "Dead Man" or Dodman), so if you wish you could go up to the road and continue via Penare back to the coast at Hemmick Beach. After about a quarter of a mile, near Penveor ("great head") Point, another track goes off, sharp right, signposted Penare; this track follows the line of the prehistoric bulwark that once defended the fort on Dodman Point (*). At the point itself, go up to the cross to get the best view seawards. This is the highest point on the south coast of Cornwall, almost 400 feet. It's also worth going a little way inland to see the little watch house, dating from 1795. Back on the coast path, the big wall on the right by the next stile marks the other end of the ancient bulwark. Next comes perhaps the toughest stretch on the walk, between High Point and Gell Point - although the path round Lambsowden Cove rivals it. After Hemmick Beach, which is described so lovingly in Anne Treneer's *School House in the Wind*, you pass Clitter's Rock - a quartzite outcrop rather similar to Carn Rocks, north of Gorran Haven - on the hill above you. The path down to Lambsowden Cove is overshadowed by an impressive row of fang-like rocks. In October the cliffs ahead were covered with bracken, brilliant rust-red. The footbridge is followed by a stiff climb; you cross a couple of unusual bridge-like stiles over hedges, and then you are round to Porthluney and a fine view of the castle. The path follows the cliff edge and joins the road where you left it earlier, just to the right of the bridge.

DODMAN POINT

Just before I came to live in Cornwall, a pleasure boat called the "Darlwin" sank off Dodman Point, drowning all her 31 passengers. At that time I had never seen the Dodman, but my mental picture was of a grim, death-ridden place, and even now when I see its forbidding black bulk in silhouette, with Parson Martin's cross like a churchyard headstone perched on its summit, I can't altogether shake off those associations. It comes as no surprise to learn that in 1699 its name was written as "Deadman Point". As so often, Anne Treneer puts it best: "Dodman absorbs the blackness of winter.... We called the Dodman, Deadman. Deadman and Vault; the names were permanent reminders of shipwreck and distress though we used them lightly and thoughtlessly enough. Yet something in Dodman subdued us. We never played there." And yet, of course, it's a place of great beauty with a power to uplift: friends of ours who live nearby say a walk on Dodman Point is the best cure for depression they know. In reality the name has nothing to do with death: Oliver Padel says it derives from the surname Dudman, and Craig Weatherhill with equal confidence states, "The name Dodman is derived from the Cornish word *tomen,* a bank or dyke." One of the most impressive features of the headland is the great Iron Age rampart, up to twenty feet high, which with an outer ditch and another lower bank runs for nearly 2,000 feet across the neck of the promontory. Within the area of nearly fifty acres thus enclosed there must have been quite a large settlement, but so far there has been no excavation to reveal the remains of dwellings; two burial mounds of an even earlier date than the Bulwark are visible, though, and so are parts of a medieval strip field system. For details about that, the watch house and the Dodman Cross, see the National Trust's *Coast of Cornwall* leaflet No. 20. When we were walking past the cottages at Tregavarras (near Caerhays) recently we chatted with a lady who wants to ensure that the approaching centenary of the cross is properly celebrated. She painted a vivid picture of the saintly Rector of Caerhays who had it set up, George Martin. Anne Treneer knew him for a short time just before "he left the secluded beauty of Caerhays to live, not as a Priest, but as a day-labourer in a London slum. He was one who took literally Christ's warning to the rich young ruler, Sell all that thou hast and give to the poor."

WALK 8
GORRAN AND MEVAGISSEY
Nearly seven miles, with a possible extension of about a mile

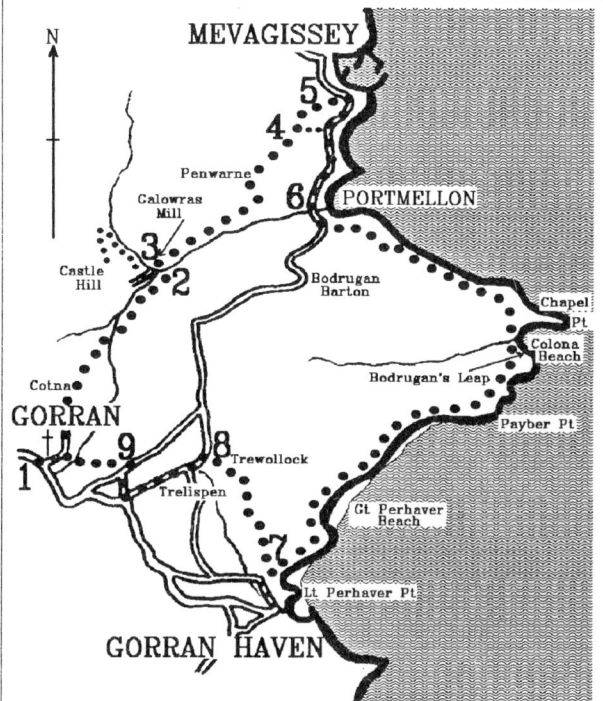

Here is yet another delightful piece of coastline, and it's probably the least strenuous to walk along of any covered in this book. I hardly need to spell out the pleasures of visiting Mevagissey and Gorran Haven; in any case, they are both included in other walks, and the main route of this one reaches only the edges of them. Almost equally enjoyable to walk through are the smaller communities of Portmellon and Gorran Churchtown. Between the latter and Mevagissey is some of the loveliest inland scenery in the region: deep, wooded, lush valleys crowned by an ancient hill fort or settlement which can be visited on a short diversion. Despite the hills, there is again nothing particularly strenuous to cope with, but mud is likely, especially around Galowras Mill. If a pub that serves palatable food is essential for a good walk, you are spoilt for choice on this one, since all four villages have at least one; and all except Portmellon also have shops that sell provisions.

The directions are given from Gorran Churchtown. Although there is no car park there, roadside parking is usually available, and by starting there you give yourself the option of not walking down into Mevagissey or Gorran Haven. This would be a particular advantage at Mevagissey, because it would enable you to reduce the amount of walking along a road which in summer can be busy. It would also avoid parking charges and reduce the risk of getting snarled up in traffic jams. To drive to Gorran from St Austell, take the B3273 south, avoiding Mevagissey by turning right about a mile north of it. Road signs should guide you safely the rest of the way, but a good map would be an advantage. From the Truro direction you could drive to it via Tregony or Grampound and Polmassick, but in either case I would regard the map as essential!

WALK 8

1 From the Barleysheaf Inn at Gorran Churchtown (*) go past the main entrance to the church and turn left. After passing a few cottages take the left turn, following the sign Public Footpath - Galowras Mill. Just before the lane reaches Cotna House, cross the stile on the right, opposite a footpath sign. Christine Hawkridge's excellent little *History of Gorran* mentions that the medieval version of "Cotna" was "Crukoner", referring to a barrow: compare "Cruggan" on Walk 8. "In 1854," she adds, "when workmen were planting the gardens of the house being built there for Mr Kendall, they discovered earthen jars filled with the charred remains of human bones." She also mentions a nearby field known as "The Plains", which may indicate the former site of a playing-place or "plain-an-gwarry". Cross the field to the stile in the centre of the hedge opposite, then bear slightly left to another stile, and after that go straight on or slightly right across the ridge to a fourth stile on the right of a gate. Now the path goes quite steeply down into this beautiful valley, keeping by the fence on the right. After crossing the stile in this fence, don't go down to the valley bottom (where, incidentally, there used to be a watermill known as Sentries Mill, apparently a corruption of "Sanctuaries": the mill stood on a piece of glebe land). Follow the footpath sign to the right, through a gate or open gap, and continue ahead beside four oak trees to a wooden stile. Next comes a path through pretty woodland. This is West Bodrugan Wood Nature Reserve; a notice on the gate at the far end requests walkers to keep to the path, walk quietly and keep dogs on leads. The pool which you pass at the start of the woodland was thickly coated with waterweed in October 1991 - "Ginny Greenteeth" was my wife's name for it, learnt from her father, a Lancashire man.

2 Immediately beyond the five-bar gate turn sharp left and cross the bridge to Galowras Mill, which was the manor mill of Galowras ("Gloeret" in the Domesday Book), about half a mile to the north. The lord of the manor's tenants would have been required to grind their corn at his mill, and in 1795 this mill had two pairs of stones for the tenants' use. The name means "clear watercourse" or "bright ford". Incidentally, when we walked here in 1988 a notice proclaimed that its owner was a Mr Grist.

You might care to make a short diversion here (less than a mile) through attractive countryside to the site of a prehistoric hilltop "castle" with fine views. If so, turn left up the narrow road beside the mill, and almost immediately turn sharp right, through a five-bar gate with a footpath sign attached. Ignore side paths, keeping at first to the grassy (in places muddy and/or cowpatted, I'm afraid) track. The old millstream or "leat", though dry now, is still clearly visible on the right side of the track. After another five-bar gate walk beside the hedge on your left. Here in October the grass was lush, and the woods in the valleys were thick and dark: a delightful scene, completed by the mill house, artistically placed at the focal point of several gentle curves. The path eventually goes down to a small stream which has created quite a large patch of mud. After negotiating that, bear left, joining a track; go through the metal gate, then turn left and go through another, back over the stream. Now the route runs gently uphill towards the hilltop trees. Go through the gap in the hedge (where there was a single strand of barbed wire to cross), then follow the clear uphill path. Soon the sea and the valley down to Portmellon come into view. At about this point

WALK 8

GORRAN CHURCHTOWN
The spelling "Gurran", used by William Wynne in his account of his travels in 1755, reflects the way the name is still often said locally, and is faithful to the earliest recorded spelling of the saint's name, "Guron". He moved here after setting up a religious community at Bodmin. Inside the large, rather empty-feeling church, perhaps the main points of interest are the collection of fifty-three 16th-century bench ends and the brass known as The Lady of Brannell. The list of vicars, near the main entrance, is also worth inspection, since it includes much more historical information than usual. In 1300 (or 1306), for example, the church was "under interdict" because the friends of a Tregony man slew his murderer in the church; in 1473 the vicar, Thomas Marbury, resigned "on account of defect of unsuitability of vulgar tongue (Cornish)"; in 1615 the vicar was "ousted for Royalist tendencies"; in 1735 the parish had 170 families, and in 1790, 400. Originally there was a spire, which was tall enough to be a navigational aid to seamen; it is shown on the back of the fine old carved chair at the east end. The spire was replaced by the present imposing tower early in the 17th century. The village seems to have changed little since last century, to judge by the old photographs. There is probably no better way to capture the flavour of life there some ninety to a hundred years ago than to read Anne Treneer's *School House in the Wind* (1944, reprinted 1983), a title which reflects the fact that the village is some 300 feet above sea-level. One change that has occurred is that the school she describes was burnt down in 1967 and rebuilt two years later.

the right of way appears to come to an end, rather frustratingly a few yards short of the hilltop, crowned by a valiant little stunted oak. From there the view is even better, including Gorran church. It is a typical site for an Iron Age hill fort, but it seems to have been a civilian settlement, despite the name, "Castle Hill". Return to the mill by the same route.

3 To continue the walk, follow the footpath sign (on the right of Galowras Mill when you first approached it), through a gate and over a footbridge: another spot that's likely to be muddy. Continue round to the right. Now the path runs down the wide valley which reaches the coast at Portmellon. Keep a few yards left of the wooded area around the stream, and then go a little further left to pass through the gap in the hedge ahead. From there the path is clear. After the next hedge, keep to the main (lowest) path, curving left behind Portmellon to Penwarne (*), a beautiful old farm with particularly impressive outbuildings. When we were last there they were being treated to several coats of bright green paint, but looked in rather more urgent need of a few hundred new rooftiles. Go through the five-bar gate and walk around the left side and front of the farmhouse to join the main drive, which brings you to a road.

> ### PENWARNE
> The name reflects the house's sheltered position: "end of the alder-marsh". From early times it belonged to the family of the same name, but during the Tudor period it passed through marriage successively to the Coswarths, the Hills and then to John Carew, second son of Richard Carew of Antony, author of the famous *Survey of Cornwall*. I'll let Polsue tell the story: "In 1601, at the siege of Ostend, this John Carew lost his right hand by a cannon ball, on which occasion he evinced considerable fortitude. Returning to his lodgings he threw the amputated hand on the table remarking to the hostess, - "this is the hand that cut the pudding to-day;" he was afterwards called *the one handed Carew*. The loss of his hand was partially supplied by a piece of mechanism curiously contrived and rendered elastic by strings; this artificial hand and his portrait were long preserved at Heligan." (Lake's *Parochial History*) (For Heligan see Walk 9.) John had only one son but many daughters, one of whom was carried off by Turkish pirates. The son left no heir; Penwarne was sold to the Fortescues, and by the time Polsue was writing most of the estate belonged to the Williams family of Caerhays. The house and outbuildings clearly retain much that is old; like The Terrace at Pentewan (Walk 6 in *Around St Austell*), Penwarne is said to include stone from the deserted mansion of Polrudden. An advert printed in *The West Briton* when Penwarne was offered for sale in 1812 included this: "The above premises are most admirably situated for manure, being within half-a-mile from Mevagissey, where town-dung may be procured in any quantity, at the low price of one shilling per butt-load, and within a quarter of a mile of Porthmellin, whence sea-sand may be brought at a trifling expense."

4 Turn left on that, and where the road bends right take the footpath almost straight ahead. *(This is the way to go if you want to include Mevagissey in the walk; and even if you don't it might still be worth it for the wonderful view over the harbour and village that it gives you. But if you would prefer to shorten the walk slightly and cut out some road walking, take the path on the right instead. This is shown on the map.)* As you approach Church Park Farm, notice the old well on the left. Go through the farm gate to the left of the house and turn right, walking downhill with the hedge on your right. After the kissing gate, go right for a few yards, past the entrance to Polhaun. Now the path goes down to the left between concrete-block walls, and you emerge on to the road above Mevagissey harbour. The temptation to walk down there will be hard to resist, especially if you're hungry and thirsty ... but bear in mind the steep hill back, and that there's a pub at Portmellon too!

5 For the coastal walk south, turn right along the road. Please walk with great care here, since it tends to be busy and there's little in the way of pavements. As you start to descend to Portmellon (*), notice the road sign, "Beware of Waves".

6 If you managed to brave the waves and have emerged unscathed, follow the acorn sign pointing left as you begin to climb the hill on the far side of

WALK 8

PORTMELLON

The name is sometimes explained as "yellow cove", but "mill cove" is more likely. There doesn't seem to be any sign of a mill there now; the fish cellars have gone, too, and so has the famous Mitchell's Boatyard (established 1922), though a sign beside the block of six new houses built on its site acts as a reminder of it. The launching slip remains, and so does an old, uprooted winch, but both look sadly redundant. The pictures on pages 24-7 of Joy Wilson's *Around St Austell Bay* tell much about Portmellon during last century and the early years of this: they recall the cholera outbreak of 1849, when 115 Mevagissey people died in five weeks and most of the surviving population occupied ordnance tents, each able to shelter 500 people, at Portmellon; they show the many fish cellars, the largest of which occupied part of what is now beach as well as the site of the blue-shuttered houses; and one is of an early car on the beach before the road was built (about 1918). The crossing is a good deal easier nowadays, except in an easterly gale, when you do indeed have to "beware of waves".

Portmellon

Portmellon. The first half-mile-or-so of the coast path here is along a made-up drive. Don't be so distracted by the glorious coastal views that you miss another acorn sign directing you to the left. Somewhere along this stretch of cliffs east of Portmellon a short-lived ochre mine called Wheal Boger was opened in 1836; for more on this topic see the later part of point 6. The clifftop path soon descends towards Chapel Point (*) and passes above Colona Beach before climbing again, past the National Trust sign, Bodrugan's Leap (*). Again, don't miss the acorn sign nearby which directs you to the left side of the wire fence, which for some distance ahead now will oblige you to keep quite close to the cliff edge. *(Some walkers may find this rather unnerving, especially round Payber Point and along the high cliffs beyond. If you would rather not risk it, you could try the inland path from above Colona Beach, which passes through Bodrugan Barton, then turn left on the road to Gorran Churchtown. I have not walked this myself; if it proves impracticable, the only other choice is to return to Portmellon by the coast path and take the road from there back to Gorran.)* About half a mile past Payber Point are the whitish, lichen-covered quartzite Carn Rocks (literally "rockpile rocks"); the path keeps to the right of them, but there's a nice little picnic or coffee-break spot on the seaward side of the first rock. From here the view to the right over the houses of Gorran Haven allows you a glimpse of the top of Dodman Point; the nearer headland beyond the village is called Pen-a-maen ("stone head"). The attractive beach you walk above next is called Great Perhaver, which Dr James Whetter thinks may mean "Harbour Cove": he speculates that "in early times" this and Little Perhaver (further south) may have been a more suitable place for Gorran harbour than

---

CHAPEL POINT

This headland was, says Sheila Bird, "capped by an ancient fort", but that is no more evident now than the medieval "lighthouse" chapel that is thought to have stood here. The chapel is sometimes said to be the one from a window of which Tristan jumped when fleeing from King Mark, foreshadowing Bodrugan's later exploit nearby. (See Joy Wilson's *Cornwall, Land of Legend,* Bossiney Books. She believes that some ruined foundation walls in the garden of the middle house are a relic of the chapel.) A different reason for the name of the point is suggested by the Mevagissey Museum's leaflet: the Mevagissey Independents (later the United Reformed Church), founded in 1626, used to hold their meetings on the headland, "where they had good warning of the approach of the authorities." The harmonious group of buildings which now occupy the site were built, largely from stones collected on Colona Beach, in the late 1930s by the architect John Campbell. His friend Frank Baker in *The Call of Cornwall* calls the three white houses "masterpieces", only part of "the celestial city that he had planned at Chapel Point - a city doomed by inane bureaucracy to live only in his imagination". "In face of all the monstrosities of domestic "architecture" which were and are blots on Cornwall's magnificent coast," declares Mr Baker, "Campbell's great work demonstrates the right way to set about it." The National Trust, choosing its adjective with great care, calls the houses "distinctive".

> ### BODRUGAN'S LEAP
> Bodrugan Barton, on the site of the Domesday manor of Bodeworgoin, is a little way inland here, still an impressive farmstead but retaining only a few bits of masonry from the great medieval manor house occupied by the family of the same name. (It was demolished in 1786.) In 1487 Henry Bodrugan, who had supported Richard III, fled, pursued by Lord Edgcumbe of Cotehele; the Edgcumbes were rewarded for their loyalty to the Lancastrian and Tudor cause by acquiring most of the Bodrugan estates. Bodrugan is supposed to have ridden his horse over the cliff. One version of the legend is that he was then taken overseas by a waiting boat, and Dr Whetter believes it is "likely" that the boat was manned by men from Portheast (Gorran Haven). Charles Causley's poem, "Young Edgcumbe", offers another ending:
>
> > And from the height, Bodrugan
> > Sprang down into the swell
> > That tide on tide at the cliff-side
> > Hammers a passing-bell.
> >
> > And ever did the ocean
> > Under Bodrugan's Leap
> > With loving care the body fair
> > Of Lord Bodrugan keep.

the present site. In 1804 an ochre mine was opened above Great Perhaver beach; at that time the ochre clay was probably quarried, but when the site was re-worked in 1897 a 40-foot shaft was sunk. An iron landing stage was built down on the beach: see photo 12 in Dr Whetter's *History of Gorran Haven*, Part 2. Dr Whetter says the ruins survive of an engine house at the point where loads of clay were lowered to the landing stage. The ochre was wanted for burnishing gold and silver, and especially for dyes and paints, but the mine closed when it was found that the clay from deeper levels yielded ochre of poor quality. The path soon descends to the bungaloid edge of Gorran Haven (*).

7 The village is well worth a visit, whether or not you want to use the pub or shops; for the pub (actually a hotel called Llawnroc: try reading it backwards) turn right at Chute Lane. But to complete the round walk without going down into the village, turn right when you reach Cliff Road, following the footpath sign to Trewollock. Now take the first right turning, and at the top of the road turn right where a footpath is marked, between the houses numbered 50 and 53. You cross two stiles, then the path runs along a slight ridge (presumably a grubbed-out hedge) with a wire fence on the right. Keep to the field edge, past a footpath sign at the corner; turn left there, go through the farm gate and walk along the track to Trewollock (or Trewollack) Farm. Keep straight on past the farm buildings, then bear left, through a wooden farm gate to the road.

8 Turn left past the front entrance to the farm, and then follow the sign to Gorran. Soon you pass Trelispen Farm, now run by Dr James Whetter as a

GORRAN HAVEN

From at least medieval times till the 18th century, Gorran was a much more important maritime community than Mevagissey (for example, in the late 16th century 68 Gorran men were listed as sailors, compared with 8 in Mevagissey). Nowadays, Mevagissey still has several working boats, whereas Gorran's fishing fleet consists of "Buccaneer", which takes visitors out fishing in summer. And yet Gorran - once you get down below the retirement villas and the car park - retains much more of the atmosphere of an old fishing and boat-building village, probably because it lacks the obvious picturesqueness of its old rival. (That rivalry sometimes flared into bitter enmity between the fishermen of Gorran and Mevagissey, as the press reported in July 1873: see *Life in Cornwall in the Late Nineteenth Century*, Bradford Barton 1972.) "Portheast" is Gorran Haven's old name, a corruption of "Porth Just": its little chapel of ease is dedicated to St Just, the same Celtic saint from whom St Just-in-Roseland and St Just-in-Penwith are named. This fascinating little building dates from the 15th century; the Chantry Act (1545-7) caused it to be deconsecrated, and then, in the words of a letter dated 1651, "the fishermen made itt a house to keep their sea tackell therein." Only in Victorian times was it fully restored and returned to use as a place of worship. A pier was built in medieval times, and Dr Whetter claims that by 1270 Gorran had "one of the largest fisheries in Cornwall". It continued to thrive, and in 1720 there were over twenty fish cellars. The harbour was improved in 1820, and in 1888 the Williams family of Caerhays had a new quay built. By then Gorran had thirty boats and sixty fishermen and was famous for boat building and crab-pot making. The limekiln building which so dominates the old village probably dates from 1812. The kilns went out of use for lime burning about 1910 and became a coal store; during the 1930s they were filled in and the top of the building became a car park. The boat pound down on the harbour beach occupies the site of "the big cellar"; next to that was a smaller fish cellar which was converted into a watch house for the preventive officers; and on the other side of the limekilns was the Ship Inn, now the Mermaid café. Photograph No. 21 in Dr Whetter's first volume gives a very clear impression of this scene in 1885. I recommend his work if you want all the details, including lots of references to particular people. Part of the flavour of the good old days is vividly evoked in his accounts of the Gorran men who during lean periods would walk to Newquay and Falmouth in search of work, and of "poor Mrs Kerkin" : "She lived in a terrible way and Henry Johns recalls ... seeing fleas coming out of her clothes by the neck and going back down again." The price for the two volumes (1991) is £17.25. For an easier read, more clearly printed, and a study which puts the salient facts into the context of the parish as a whole, go for Christine Hawkridge's *A History of Gorran*, if it can still be had. That cost 40p in 1988. *The Cornwall Village Book*, produced by the W.I. in 1991, has some interesting "snippets", such as the fact that Rattle Street is so called because it used to be cobbled, and that the name of the owner of the general-store-cum-bakery is Cakebread.

WALK 8

"Camping Park" and a Craft Centre. Cream Teas were advertised, but this was October and everything was firmly shut down till next season. Dr Whetter thinks "Trelispen" might mean "farm at the end of the court", though there is no evidence that the Bodrugan manorial courts were held there. When you reach the main road (Bell Hill), turn sharp right along a minor road marked "Unsuitable for Motors". At the T-junction turn right, and after about a hundred yards cross the stile on the left, where there is a footpath sign to St Goran's Church.

9 Now go left, heading roughly towards the church tower. Cross a stile over a wall and continue ahead with the hedge on your right. At the bottom, cross the muddy patch around the stream by means of a few stepping-stones (a bit of corrugated iron also helped!) to a stile with "Footpath" painted on it. Cross that with care: the block on the far side is a bit insecure. Go round by the cottage and at the road turn left for the church, shop and pub.

Gorran Haven

WALK 9
MEVAGISSEY, HELIGAN MILL AND PENTEWAN SANDS
About four miles

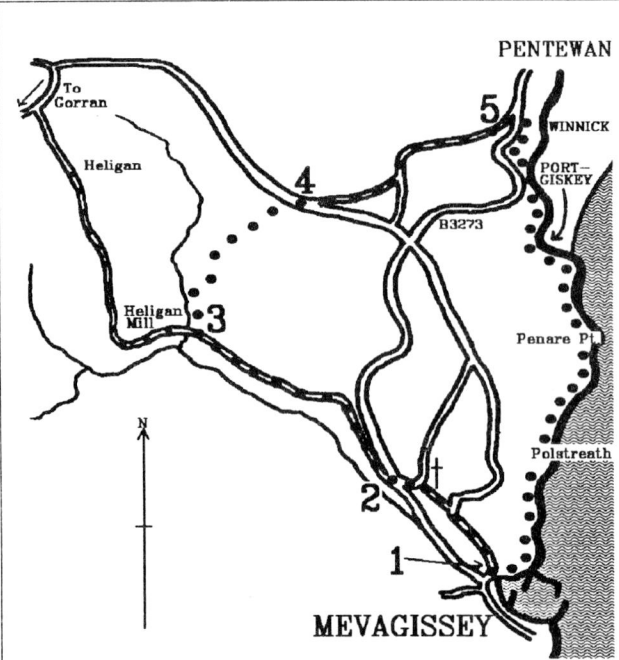

This walk begins with one of the most beautiful valleys in the area and ends with a very fine stretch of coast path. Among many other delights, it gives you unrivalled birds'-eye views of both Pentewan and Mevagissey. In fact, if you have never been to Mevagissey before doing this walk, perhaps you should consider starting the walk at Pentewan, just so that your very first sight of Mevagissey will be from the coast path on the north side - though I must admit that the view from the top of Polkirt Hill, included on Walk 8, is hardly less memorable. Other special attractions include a deserted fishing hamlet - a particularly magical place - and a grand country mansion set among woods. Its garden, once among the most important in Cornwall, is currently being rescued from decades of neglect, and there is talk of its being open to the public in 1992. A short diversion from this walk would provide an ideal opportunity to visit it. I mustn't pretend that the walk is an easy one, because there are steep slopes both inland and along the coast. The farm tracks are likely to be muddy, and the woodland paths may sometimes be rather overgrown. There are several rather high stiles to cross, and one gate had to be climbed when we did the walk. About half a mile of the route is along roads which at times carry quite fast traffic. The only pubs and other "facilities" are in Mevagissey, unless you extend the walk by about half a mile in order to visit Pentewan, which would make a good pausing-place at about the half-way point. If the weather invites bathing, try Polstreath Beach, close to Mevagissey.

Directions are given from the Market Square in Mevagissey (*).

MEVAGISSEY

Just as at Gorran and Gerrans, a village developed here around a church on high ground inland, and another clustered around the nearest sea-cove. In this case they were rather closer together, but the distinctness of their identities in early times is illustrated by the fact that they had different names: the churchtown and parish were "Lammorek" (meaning "church by the sea", perhaps) in the 13th century - later modified to "Levorrick" - and the harbour community was Porthilly (possibly "brine cove"). An alternative name for the churchtown by about 1400 was a combination of the names of the two saints to whom the church was dedicated, "Memai and Iti", later called "Meva et Ida" or "Meva and Issey"; a relic of the Cornish word for "and", *hag,* explains the g in "Mevagissey". It's surprising that this became the name for the whole village, since it was Porthilly that grew and prospered as a boat-building and fishing community. The basis of what is now the inner harbour was built in 1430; the great days of Mevagissey as a port, however, came some three centuries later. In the 1770s the outer harbour and many other additions were made, and if further proof of the village's importance were needed the existence by then of at least ten pubs surely clinches it. A visitor in 1824 claimed that "as a fisher town, Mevagizzey ranks before any other in the county" (F.W.L.Stockdale); but only 18 years later Cyrus Redding's comment was, "This was one of the most noted fishing towns in Cornwall, until the visits of the pilchard to its shores became less frequent." "The streets are wretchedly narrow," he adds; "and from this cause the fish are obliged to be carried in baskets to the cellars, between two men with poles over their shoulders. Mevagissy contains some good houses, and the interior of the humblest is remarkable for its cleanliness: yet the odour of the fish is not prevented from being perceptible to the stranger. The fishermen are a fine, active and daring race of men, trained to hardship from their boyhood." The personal stories of the descendants of those men and their families in the first few decades of this century have been remembered in amazing detail by Mary Lakeman in *Early Tide;* and the atmosphere of the place in 1937 is captured perhaps even more vividly by Frank Baker in *The Call of Cornwall:* "The shops were real shops; that is to say, ... you could buy the side of a pig at the drapery by the post office (probably kept under a bed upstairs by Mr Farren), vegetables at Mr Rowe's the butcher's, and everything from a pin to a lawnmower at Mr Rowse's the ironmonger's, opposite The Ship. The narrow little streets were still cobbled. Water came from the green pump between Mr Rowse's and The Ship. The flush lavatory was only in the better houses. Early every morning the human load was carried in buckets to chutes tunnelled into the rock-sides above the harbour." Not just the odour of fish was perceptible to the stranger. Well, he is catered for more than adequately now, and the dedication to the tourist trade of what was once a self-sufficient community provokes sadness in Miss Lakeman and bitter anger in Mr Baker. But fishing and boatbuilding continue, and there's still a great deal of the old Mevagissey to enjoy. In your exploration of the village you can't do better than take with you the Heritage Coast's *Mevagissey Walkabout* and Peter Bray's collection of old photographs, *Around & About Mevagissey.*

WALK 9

1 Start by walking away from the harbour, along Church Street. This takes you past The Loft, the only specialist bookshop in the town, which stocks all the available books about this area, by which you can plug all or most of the gaps that have to be left in a book that is meant to be portable! Further up the road, watch for the blue sign to the church (on the left), and follow it. This minor road soon brings you to the south gate of the churchyard. Do visit the church (*) if you have time. To continue the walk, go past the "No Entry" signs, along a lane that brings you to the main road.

2 Cross that with care and turn right along a wide path (almost a minor road, in fact: cars use it) which at first runs parallel with the road. Soon you are walking up the delightful valley leading to Heligan. Between the first and second farm gates you are on a rough track, still running up the right side of the valley. The third gate, a smaller, metal one with a slate stile beside it, brings you to a footbridge.

3 Immediately before the bridge the main walk route turns right, following the narrow path up into the woods - but first it's worth going ahead along the main track for a few more yards to look at Heligan Mill. It was here that some members of what Frank Baker calls "our little art colony" lived during the 1940s: see *The Call of Cornwall*. The mill itself is the building on the left just past a comparatively modern cottage. A millstone lies near the water tank; the waterwheel was against the right-hand end wall of the building, and the remains of the leat are on the left side of the main track as it continues uphill.   (An old photograph of Heligan Mill is on page 78.)

To visit the garden at Heligan House (*), if and when it opens to the public, go on up that track for about a further half mile. Ivor Herring, in an article in "Cornish Garden", 1983, referring to the grounds of Heligan in Victorian and Edwardian times, writes that "a visitor recalled you could walk from Heligan Mill to the house in carpet slippers, the paths being so well kept." At that period, the route may have been through the Japanese Garden in the valley; during the time of the Tremaynes the people of Mevagissey were permitted to walk up through that on Sunday afternoons. Nowadays you might need a machete there - and even on the track those carpet slippers would do well to survive the journey.

The first part of the woodland path up from the footbridge looks as if it may get overgrown at times, but we had no problems with it in September 1991. Soon it becomes an attractive sunken path; presumably it was once a farm track or narrow lane down to the mill. One section, where it runs between open fields, is quite steep uphill; then it levels off as it runs along the left edge of more woodland, and here two or three fallen trees necessitated first a small diversion to the right and then a little ducking and crawling. At the end of the woods, go through the gate and follow the direction shown by the yellow arrow on it, keeping beside the hedge on your right. Here you have a beautiful view of wooded valleys, with the Georgian Heligan House prominent. The tractor track brings you to a road via a gate (padlocked when we were there) just to the right of an electricity sub-station.

4 Turn right on the road. PLEASE TAKE CARE ON THIS BUSY ROAD, and walk facing the oncoming traffic. Luckily, you don't have to stay on it for long: take the minor road on the left, marked "Unsuitable for Heavy Goods Vehicles", and then at the T-junction turn left. This rather wider road is used

MEVAGISSEY CHURCH

As you enter the churchyard on the south side, notice at ground level on your right the three old gravestones made from sea boulders; two of them are clearly dated. The story behind the unusual tower is that the original one was demolished in the 17th century and not replaced till Victorian times. Two pinnacles from the old tower have been used to decorate the gate-posts at the north entry to the churchyard. The sundial above the main door dates from 1713 and is said to bear a punning inscription, but we found it totally illegible. There is undoubtedly, however, a good crop of puns inside, on the impressive slate monument, dated 1632, mounted on the wall near the north altar. The Dart family - father, mother, two large daughters and six small sons - are all depicted, but the ingenious verses refer to the deaths of only the father and three sons:

> Death shoots sometimes as archers doe,
> One Darte to finde another;
> But now by shooting hath founde fovr,
> And all layd hear together. ....
>
> The warfar past the Darts must rest;
> This grave shall be the quiver,
> Where they shall rest till with the blest,
> They be revived for ever.

Another memorial worth study is that to Otwell Hill and his wife (1617), near the main altar. The pillars dividing the two aisles are of Pentewan stone (see Walk 6 in *Around St Austell),* but the central one is a 19th-century replacement; the original fell, and was for a time used in the Mevagissey clink to hold prisoners' chains. It is now in the town's museum. There are a few traces of the original Norman church, and the font is probably Norman or only a little later in date; otherwise, the older parts of the church are mostly 15th century. "It was old until J. P. St Aubyn got at it," is John Betjeman's response to the efforts of that doyen of Victorian restorers of Cornish churches. Even its picturesque ancient dedication to Saints Meva and Ida has been supplanted by St Peter, but I don't think Mr St Aubyn can be blamed for (or credited with) that.

HELIGAN HOUSE AND GARDEN

Heligan (said, at least by the purists, with the stress on the second syllable) means "willow-tree". The old manor has belonged to the Tremayne family since the 16th century. Little remains of the house they built in 1603 and improved in 1692, because it was almost wholly rebuilt in 1809-10 and thus became "one of the handsomest and most commodious mansions of the county" (Lake's *Parochial History*). The house had a long drive from the Pentewan Valley; you can still trace much of its course of the OS map, and see where it passed under the road near Peruppa Farm. As far back as 1650 the Tremaynes began developing a magnificent 22-acre garden, and by about 1910 there were walled gardens, peach houses, melon grounds, an Italian Garden, a Japanese Garden, a wishing well, a summer house, a grotto, an area called "Flora's Green" where the ladies of the house are said to have danced, one of Britain's largest and finest sets of bee-boles (recesses in a wall, used to give shelter to straw bee-skeps before moveable-frame bee-hives were introduced into Britain in 1862) - and most important of all, a superb collection of plants, many of them introduced by a famous Victorian plant-hunter, Sir Joseph Hooker. The rhododendrons at Heligan were particularly celebrated. From about 1900 the "new garden" was developed, and this attracted a visit by King George V and Queen Mary. (A further royal connection according to local belief is that Heligan was considered as a possible home for the Duke of Windsor and Mrs Simpson.) The Tremaynes have not lived there since World War I, when the house became a hospital; then it was let to a succession of tenants, and now it is divided into some twenty flats. The male line of the Tremaynes ceased in 1949. The garden has, for the most part, been allowed to run wild for at least the last fifty years. Frank Baker described the "riot of vegetation" in *The Call of Cornwall* (1976): "Decaying woods where sprawling rhododendrons clutch out above the fallen trunks of ash and willow, monstrous fungi, blackberries large as solitaire marbles, sunflowers five feet high, thickets buzzing with insects and shimmering in the lazy flight of butterflies ...." In September 1991 it was the subject of a BBC-2 documentary entitled "The Lost Garden", in which it was described as a time-capsule. In recent years, much work has been done - mainly on the borders nearest the house but also elsewhere in the garden - by the occupants of one of the flats, Ivor and Maisie Herring, and now an ambitious project to restore the whole garden is under way, thanks largely to the energy and enthusiasm of Tim Smit, a former rock-and-roll producer who came from London with the intention of setting up a studio in Cornwall, but instead fell in love with "the lost garden". With the help of a management team, local people and the British Trust for Conservation Volunteers, rapid progress is being made, and there are hopes of opening the garden to the public in the spring of 1992. Although like most Cornish gardens it is likely to be most spectacular in spring, there are many plants of year-round interest, such as giant tree-ferns from South Australia, and indeed there is a possibility that Heligan will be chosen as the setting for the British national collection of hardy ferns. (Incidentally, you may be interested to know that the Dower House at Heligan became the home of the author E.V.Thompson in 1978.)

by some fast traffic, so please again be very careful: don't be too distracted by the view of Pentewan and Black Head. Eventually you come down to the main St Austell - Mevagissey road.

5 *To visit Pentewan, turn left on the main road, and then right.* To return to Mevagissey, cross the road and take the path on the right at the entrance to the Pentewan Sands Caravan Park. This occupies an area of low dunes known as The Winnick, which was also an old name for the St Austell River. The Winnick used to be a good place for picnics and games, and it attracted day-trippers such as those on Sunday School outings before World War I, who were brought down by rail from St Austell in cleaned-out china-clay wagons. (See A.L.Rowse's *A Cornish Childhood.*) I believe there are now plans to move the mobile homes further inland and restore the old character of the place. The path, which by now you have probably forgotten I mentioned, leads up to the main road and then continues as the coast path, still running beside the road for a few hundred yards. Cross the stile on your left, and now the path takes you to the cliffs and quite steeply down to the ruins of Portgiskey (*), which you can explore by crossing another stile and

---

PORTGISKEY

The Tremaynes of Heligan for many years kept their boat at this cove, and employed a boatman who lived here. When the pilchard fishery in the west of England was at its height, in the 18th and early 19th centuries, a small community dependent on fishing and boatbuilding flourished at Portgiskey. Now only these poignant ruins remain as evidence of the cottages and their gardens, the pilchard cellars, the quay .... Even Port Quin, which according to the legend repeated by all the guide books was abandoned after all the menfolk were drowned in one terrible storm, lacks something of the atmosphere of this place, if only because the National Trust has provided a car park there and made the old cellars and cottages into holiday accommodation. The magic of Portgiskey prompted E.V.Thompson to use it as a setting in his novels *The Restless Sea* and *Polrudden.*

Portgiskey

taking a side path. The coast path now crosses a footbridge and three stiles and takes you on a long, stiff climb to Penare Point. (This is one of three places called Penare or Pennare in the area covered by this book; see the note on Nare Head in Walk 5.) One consolation as you climb is the magnificent cliff scenery close at hand (but don't twist your ankle in a badger-hole as you look at it); and at the top you have first a splendid view of Pentewan and the coast to Black Head, and then a delightful one ahead over Mevagissey and Portmellon to Chapel Point. Next there is a descent towards the attractive Polstreath ("stream-pool"?) Beach; the coast path stays well above it, but still there is another quite stiff climb before you reach a short flight of steps at the edge of Mevagissey. Go straight on across the playing field and down past the Coastguard Station to the harbour. To find the Mevagissey Museum, on Island Quay, turn sharp left at the bottom. It is open from Easter to October each year. One of the best village museums I know, it deserves at least a couple of hours of your time. The building itself, dating from 1745, is worth study, retaining as it does many features of the boatbuilder's shop it originally was: the big old lathe is still in the joiner's shop, for example. Among the larger exhibits are an apple crusher, a cider press, a horse-operated barley thresher, and the one which gets most attention from visitors, a complete Cornish kitchen. In addition there is, of course, a huge  collection of small items which is constantly being added to. "There is always something new to see", as the leaflet says; and the people who run the Museum are local-history enthusiasts who will probably be able to answer all the questions about Mevagissey that a small book like this has to ignore.

Heligan Mill as shown on a postcard of about 1900. (See page 74.)

WALK 10
ST EWE AND POLMASSICK

A little under four miles, or there are shorter versions.

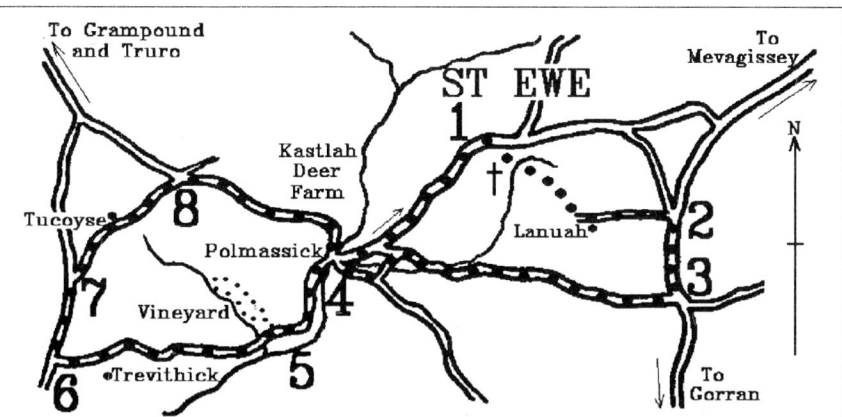

This short inland walk would be ideal for wet-weather conditions, because most of it is on minor roads; one section uses a field path and a farm track, but a route along roads could be substituted for that. The main points of interest are two delightful and unspoilt old villages, one of which has a church well worth visiting; and a vineyard in a beautiful valley. The vineyard is open to the public during the season, and in addition to strolling around the grounds you can get refreshments there - and buy the wine. The countryside is very pleasing: rolling hills cut through with many little wooded valleys and studded with sturdy old farm buildings. Most of the farms have "diversified" to some extent - by offering holiday accommodation, for example, and in one case by stocking its fields with deer. The walk is generally easy, but there is one quite long climb. A few short stretches of road are likely to be moderately busy at the height of the holiday season. Toilets as well as refreshments are available at the vineyard (Polmassick), and there is a very appealing pub at St Ewe. As this is a figure-of-eight walk, you could easily cut out half of it if you wish, for example by starting and ending at the vineyard, thus covering only sections 5 to 7 and the start of 8 in the directions.

The Crown Inn at St Ewe and the Polmassick Vineyard both have car parks for customers, and it is usually possible to park near the church, but in that case please try to avoid times of services. St Ewe, some three miles west of Mevagissey, is signposted to the right on the road from St Austell to Gorran; driving from Truro you could take a right turning on leaving Grampound and, with the aid of a map, approach St Ewe via Polmassick.

1 From St Ewe Church (*), I suggest you start by trying the one part of the walk which may give rise to problems, namely the field path to Lanuah farm.

ST EWE CHURCH

When I taught at Falmouth School I became acquainted with the eloquent and erudite vicar of Budock, the Rev. John Rham, now Canon Rham. The fact that his previous incumbency had been that of St Ewe appealed to my sense of humour as much as to his own. I wonder if it ever found its way into one of those little books with titles like *Strange but True* or *Funny Peculiar*. According to Oliver Padel's *Cornish Place Names*, St Ewe the person was probably, as you might expect, female, but that's about all anyone seems to know. The name of the nearby farm, Lanuah, means "St Ewe's church-place", and it confirms that that saint's name was originally two syllables, "Euwa" or "Ywa"; the village name, however, is locally pronounced "St Tue", and appears in 16th- and 17th-century documents as "Twe" and "St Tew". The glory of the church is the intricately carved rood screen, said in the church guide leaflet to be "the only one of its kind and age in Cornwall to have escaped destruction by Cromwell's soldiers". It's a pity the church is so dark inside that it's difficult to make the "close inspection" recommended by the leaflet; John Betjeman lays the blame for that on the much-maligned J.P.St Aubyn, who restored the church in Victorian times. If you need help with interpreting the details on the screen, Arthur Mee's *Cornwall* is a useful supplement to the church guide. In addition there are several interesting monuments, a Norman font, an old wagon roof in the south aisle, and old carved bench-ends incorporated in the pulpit. Ivor Herring (see the note on Heligan, Walk 9) has made a copy of the 1676 seating plan, now displayed in the church. It is worth close study for the light it sheds on Cornish society at that period. One interesting point is that most, but not quite all, of the wives were segregated from their menfolk in church. Mr Herring has contributed an interesting article about this seating plan to the Autumn 1991 edition of *Old Cornwall*. He also mentions that St Ewe is unusual among Cornish churches in having a broached spire, that is, an octagonal spire with a square pyramidal base. Near the gate is the tombstone of Hugh Atwell, rector of St Ewe (d. 1617), whose skill in "Phisike" (medicine) was commended by Carew in the *Survey of Cornwall*. Even apart from the fact that "his iudgment in urines commeth little behind the skilfullest in that profession", he was unusual in prescribing milk and apples rather than relying on blood-letting. Among many other virtues, Carew also praises his "liberalitie": "on the poore he bestoweth his paines & charges *gratis*."

WALK 10

You need good watertight boots for it unless the weather has been unusually dry, and at the very start you may need a stick to cope with nettles and other vegetation. *(If all that sounds too off-putting, you could instead walk east on the road towards Mevagissey; that is, from the church go past the pub. Ignore the left turning, towards St Austell, but take the first turning on the right, which comes after about a quarter of a mile. This minor road brings you to Beacon Cross; pick up the directions at point 2.)* For the footpath, walk through the churchyard on the east (left) side of the church. A path leads to the left-hand corner, where you may have to knock nettles aside in order to reach some steps that lead down to an old pump in a hollow. A couple more steps up on the other side of the hollow bring you to a barbed-wire fence, but you should be able to get round that to the left by pushing back a few branches. Step across the stream - I hope it won't be too wide for that - and go a few yards left to where it's quite easy to climb the far bank. Now walk up the field, just left of the top of the ridge. When the buildings of Lanuah come into view, head for the one furthest right. Go through the five-bar wooden gate, then walk up beside the hedge on your left and through another gate, where you turn left to pass among the old farm buildings, and continue ahead along the rather muddy farm lane to join the road at Beacon Cross.

2 Turn right there. (The reasons for the name are soon obvious: an ancient Cornish cross stands beside a small layby opposite, and the view eastward includes a long stretch of coast, with the daymark at Gribbin Head prominent, so presumably beacon fires were once lit here. The cross is described by A.G.Langdon in *Old Cornish Crosses* under the name of Corran.) This road can be busy at times, so please take care.

3 At the crossroads, where there are signs left to Kestle (one of seven Cornish places so named; it can mean "castle" or "fort", but might be just a "settlement"), turn right. This unsignposted back-road - no more than a lane - runs gently downhill most of its length, with a charming little valley to the left, and later it gives a good view ahead of Polmassick hamlet and the woods above it. You could take the even narrower road (known as Drunkards' Lane) on the left beside a bungalow called Sunny Corner (unless the name has changed now - always a danger when giving directions); this goes beside some derelict cottages. One of them is apparently being considered for restoration; called Bunny's Cottage, it is named after a "freelance" farmworker who is still remembered locally. Turn right at the T-junction, and soon you will reach the crossroads at Polmassick, where the River Luney passes under a pretty two-arched bridge on its way to the cove which bears its name, overlooked by Caerhays Castle. The name "Polmassick" means "Madek's bridge", *pons* having become *pol*. The name of one of the cottages shows that there was formerly a mill here.

4 You could return direct to St Ewe by turning right; but for the complete walk turn left, where a board announces Polmassick Vineyard. Rather strangely in this lovely spot, the ground on the left has been allowed to become the industrial world's answer to the elephants' graveyard: a place where old lorries and JCBs come to die. You can soon forget that, however, as you turn up the short drive beside a converted chapel to the vineyard (*).

WALK 10

> ### POLMASSICK VINEYARD
> Described by its present owners as "Cornwall's first commercial vineyard", it was begun in 1978 when Müller Thurgau and Seyve Villard vines were planted. The first commercial crop (two tons) was harvested in 1983, and since then several other varieties of grape have been tried. At any time of year you can buy bottles of wine, but to tour the grounds, sample wines by the glass and get refreshments (mainly ploughman's lunches and cream teas) you need to come between the second May Bank Holiday weekend and the last Sunday in September, 11 am to 5 pm - not Mondays apart from Bank Holidays. One of the biggest attractions is the delightful little walk you can do: it runs near the bottom of a very pretty wooded valley, where a cow, a calf and a Falabella pony called Vino introduced themselves to us, and returns to the Winery at a higher level along a grassy track that is shown on some old maps as a road. Seats are strategically placed to help you to enjoy the views.

5 To continue the walk on leaving the vineyard, turn right and go on up the valley road. Kilbol House looked a delightful spot for a quiet holiday; so too in its very different way did Trevithick Barton, described as a 16th-century farmhouse offering en suite accommodation, which stands at the top of the long hill. The hedges are high up here, but a gateway on the left gives you a view of the coast, presumably at Porthluney.

6 At the T-junction turn right. Take care on this rather busy road.

7 Take the first right turning, signposted "Polmessick". Tucoyse ("woodside") farm is yet another which now caters for the visitors, the old barns having been attractively converted into "holiday cottages" in a pleasant setting, complete with duckpond. Tucoyse Manor is listed in the Domesday Book as "Ticoith".

8 At the T-junction turn right. From here you get a glimpse of St Ewe spire. The road descends back into the Polmassick valley, with tall trees overshadowing mossy, ferny banks which I would guess are smothered in primroses and bluebells earlier in the year. Towards the bottom of the hill you may catch sight of a few deer in the fields to the left, part of the herd of Kastlah Deer Farm. At the Polmassick crossroads go left, following the signs to St Ewe and the Crown Inn. Soon you have quite wide valley views to the left, and can get an impression of the size of the Kastlah herd. The stone and slate-hung houses and the deserted-looking farm on this side of St Ewe superficially appear to be older than most of the buildings close to the church; maybe that's why the latter have to proclaim their antiquity by their names: The Old Stables, The Old Pottery House, The Old School House .... Unfortunately, what might have been a useful shop is now The Old Post Office. Luckily the pub is just a few yards away. That's old too, and so is some of its furniture, especially the wonderful curved, high-backed oak settle beside the oak fireplace with its pewter pots and dishes. We found the menu good and the welcome friendly. The little building in the pub's car park was originally St Ewe's clink, where offenders spent the night before being taken to the nearest police station. The small square in front of the church was once the village market-place, and the stone centre-piece formerly served as a mounting block. The column at the centre may possibly be the remains of an old cross; it used to be crowned with a sundial.

St Ewe

Coffee stop overlooking Porthbean Beach (Walk 4)